You Touched My Life

Bishop Carlis Moody is a man of all seasons and a symbol of hope to those he serves. During the course of my ministry life, he has been a mentor, counselor, teacher and a father. He has consistently responded to ministry needs around the world with dignity and the heart of 'The Good Shepherd'. This book is a "must" read!

Dr. Tony Williams, Sr.
Maranatha Christian Center
San Jose, California

Bishop Moody is one of the finest examples of a Bishop in Christendom. He is a genuine man of faith with a sincere passion for soul-winning, discipleship, and leadership development. I love Bishop Moody's God-given humility, his steadfastness and commitment to holiness. Bishop Moody's life and testimonies have impacted me in a profound way, which has positively affected my ministry and walk with God. This book will encourage the faint-hearted.

Dr. Astead N. Herndon
Hallelujah Temple
Park Forest, Illinois

Bishop Moody has been and continues to be a man of God who has rigorously studied God's Word and diligently applied it in his life. Bishop Moody, as a pastor and shepherd for over fifty years, has passionately taught the Word of God to the people of God by precept and example. This book will give the reader a glimpse of the power of God in operation.

Deacon Jerry Williams
Faith Temple COGIC
Evanston, Illinois

Chuck and I met Bishop Carlis L. Moody in 1982 on a trip to the World Pentecostal Convention in Nairobi, Kenya. Since that time, we have found him to be a man of God. Because he truly possesses the fruit of the spirit, we and our brothers and sisters in Christ worldwide, revere him. He truly has a story to tell.

Brother Chuck & Dr. June Rivers
Antioch COGIC
Detroit, Michigan

Dear Bishop Moody (Dad):
Mother Smith, your mother, told me stories of how she held me as a baby in Winter Park, Florida. The Lord knew back then in the early 1940s that I would need someone to guide me and teach me His ways, so he planted you in my life. God orchestrated our paths to cross years later in Illinois. Thank you for being faithful to Him and always living the life you have preached about through the years. What an example you and Mother Moody have been for Evelyn and me ~ Psalm 37:23 & 37. WE LOVE AND APPRECIATE BOTH OF YOU! (Your Children)

Bishop Lorenzo L. and Evelyn A. Kelly
Faith Temple COGIC
Rapid City, South Dakota

As a Father, Bishop Moody has taught us the Word of God and the Law of Life. The wisdom and holiness of his life command us to live for Christ. Psalm 78:5-6 states it best: "For He established a testimony in Jacob, and appointed a law in Israel, which He commanded our fathers, that they should make them known to their children: That the generation to come might know them, even the children which should be born; who should arise and declare them to their children:" I remain the son of My Father.

Pastor Mel Cartwright
New Family Life COGIC
North Chicago, Illinois

Bishop, you are a spiritual father, a cherished friend, and an example in word, conversation, charity, spirit, faith, and purity. My family and I are blessed because of your dedicated service to the Lord. The life of each reader will be blessed to share your story.

Elder A.L. Perryman and Family
Harvest Temple COGIC
Evanston, Illinois

Bishop Moody (Dad):

I honor you as a man for all seasons. You have been the central figure reflecting the love and faithfulness of Christ through the many seasons of my life naturally and spiritually. Your fathering has given me countless memories and numerous blessings to treasure. You provided me the chance to fulfill the prophetic call on my life. I've willingly followed your steps, always knowing that they would lead to life. I marked the perfect man, and that man was and is you! Dad, you taught me to 'Trust in the Lord'; not only as you sang it, but as you lived it through the many experiences I witnessed. You showed me that no matter what comes, it was possible to stay on the battlefield...even when wounded. Praise God for the example! Bishop, you preached the Word of God without compromise and lived a life that was blameless when it seemed that many were falling on every side. I resented how so many called you father. I didn't understand why so many grown men still needed someone to call Dad. Year by year and season by season, you clearly and steadily showed me what I had not experienced in the natural; the mentoring and the reassurance of an earthly father. The season came and still remains where you are the only man that I am honored and deeply humbled to call my father and Dad. You have shown the grace and wisdom of God by always speaking the words of life; and when life brought the most difficult circumstances and tests, you remained the same and stayed consistent in your advice and counsel.

For these and so many other reasons, I honor and respect you and I rise to call you "A Man and a Father for all seasons!"

Your Son,
Lyle Q. Foster
"One of the Sons of the Temple"
The Worship Center
Evanston, Illinois

One thing I often say is that, "Good preachers are a dime a dozen; but men of God are few and far between." One of the most impressive things about Bishop Moody is that 'his life is a reflection of righteousness.' I've traveled with him, my wife and I stayed in his home, I've eaten at his table, I've shared in his church, I've seen him up close, and I've admired him from a distance. I can say without doubt that he has been one of the greatest examples of godliness that I have found in any man. I am so privileged because he has influenced my life and has mentored me in the things of God.

Bishop Darrell L. Hines
Senior Pastor/Founder
Christian Faith Fellowship Church
Milwaukee, Wisconsin

Bishop Moody is a man of indomitable courage, impeccable integrity, matchless grace and immense wisdom. If there is one book besides the bible that you read this year, let it be this one. Reference it often and let it serve as a template for your mission in life.

Elder Delroy Hewitt
ORU, Victory Christian Center
Tulsa, Oklahoma

Bishop Carlis Moody, whom I consider my spiritual father and mentor, is the man I most admire in ministry. He is the epitome of genuine love, humility and wisdom. I consider myself more than blessed to have him as an example of an impeccable leader.

Pastor Clifford Wilson
Mount Pisgah
Evanston, Illinois

I was blessed to sit under the leadership of Bishop Moody for more than ten years. His transparency, family oriented teachings, and faithfulness helped to shape my life and ministry. Bishop Moody has been instrumental in helping me to understand and endure adversity, live with integrity and preach with authority. I consider him to be both a father and a friend.

Pastor Ivan Hartsfield
Faith Covenant Fellowship
Schaumburg, Illinois
Williams Bay, Wisconsin

It gives me the greatest pleasure to share how Bishop Carlis L. Moody, Sr. has influenced my life and ministry. As a Pastor, I have used some of the same wisdom that he used and as a result, my ministry has been successful. When he would go out to preach, he always determined that he would come back saved. His words are still with me today. "I am determined to come back saved." He showed great patience toward people that were not really saved. He gave them a chance to get their lives together. As members of Faith Temple, we were taught to trust God's word and to pay tithes. I took a step of faith based on his teaching and example. His love for missions has been one of the greatest influences in my life.

Pastor Herbert Hoffman
Abundant Life Ministry
Chicago, Illinois

HUMILITY *before* HONOUR

HUMILITY *before* HONOUR

The fear of the Lord is the instruction of
wisdom; and before honour is humility.
Proverbs 15:33

BISHOP CARLIS LEE MOODY, SR.
WITH RENA M. BOSTON

Unless otherwise indicated, all scripture quotations are from the
King James Version of the Bible

Printed in the United States of America by:
Mall Graphics, Inc.
5731 West Howard Street
Niles, Illinois 60714
877.203.2453

Cover and Book Design by: **Open Arms**
Cover Art © May 1, 1997 Richard Stewart Halstead

CD © 2005~Written and Produced by:
Edward E. Jackson
Kenneth L. Daniel, Sr.

Wedding Poem © 2005 Written by: **June Huff**

Some names have been changed throughout the book.

ISBN 0-9727848-4-5

For licensing/copyright information, additional copies or use in specialized
settings contact:

Just Writers Publishing Company
C/O Faith Temple COGIC
P.O. Box 733
Evanston, IL 60204
faithtemple@ameritech.net
(847) 328-3808 (Telephone)
(847) 328-3925 (Fax)

DEDICATION

This book is dedicated to 'Baby', Mary Alice Moody, my beloved wife of 50 years. Baby has always been my strongest supporter and prayer partner. During times of discouragement, she was always by my side encouraging me and sharing her strength. Even in the struggles to produce this book, she has under-girded me with her love. I will never be able to repay her for what she has been to me, *my helpmeet*. Thank you 'Baby'.

A special thanks to my children, Sideary, Carlis Jr., Anthony Charles Sr., and Jeffrey, without your roles in my life, my story would be limited. My desire is that you would extend the legacy that I have begun.

In loving memory of my mother, Geneva Smith, who gave me life. I will always love you.

'HONEY'

Honey:

There is not enough time or space to express everything that has made our life so special. I must, however, share with you the gratitude that is in my heart.

Come back with me fifty years when we began our life as one:

- *We married young, but our love sustained us through the challenges of life.*
- *We shared the lean times when finances were very low.*
- *We experienced the loss of everything as our home went up in smoke.*
- *We withstood the hard times while establishing the church, but today we rejoice in its growth and glory.*
- *We experienced the agony and joy of child rearing, but through our ups and downs our oneness was our stability.*

In the midst of everything, God, who worketh all things after the counsel of His own will, called you to the mission field. This required extensive travel and absence from home. We were together in spirit, but the 'homecomings' were always memorable.

The day came when the children were grown and I was able to join you on some of your missionary journeys:

- **You and me,** *exploring foreign lands such as Mexico, Hong Kong, Bermuda, Puerto Rico, Singapore, Japan, and the Philippines.*
- *We walked together on the Jericho Wall, visited Mount Olivet, stepped in the Jordan River, and witnessed what is believed to be the birth site of Jesus.*
- *Together we saw the riches of Sweden, the poverty of the Dominican Republic, and the eyes of poor children in Haiti.*
- *In Rome, we basked in the beauty of St. Peter's Cathedral, observing the masterful artwork of Michael Angelo. We also enjoyed the opportunity to hear a sermon from Pope John Paul II.*
- *In London, we sampled English tea in the Queen's palace.*
- *We traveled the white ski slopes of Switzerland and Norway.*
- *We challenged church growth in Hawaii and the Bahamas.*
- *We visited the memorable castles, windmills, and concentration camps throughout Germany.*
- *Hand in hand, we strolled along the beaches in the Caribbean.*
- *Together, we beheld the Eiffel Tower of Paris,* **you and me.**

These memories are most precious!

In you, God has given me bountiful blessings:

- *You are my* **BISHOP,** *with strength of character to face challenges and courage to rise above adversities.*
- *You are my* **PASTOR,** *who unselfishly gives himself to God's people.*
- *You are a* **FATHER,** *for our children. You are every thing it means to be a father, a provider, a role model, and a godly example.*
- *You are a* **FRIEND** *that only God can surpass.*
- *You are a loving* **HUSBAND,** *who is caring and dedicated, first to God and then to me. I will forever cherish your continual practice of holding my hand and diligently praying with and for me nightly.*

*I am happy to take my place beside you, because today and always, it will forever be '**You and Me'.**

Love Always,
Baby

ACKNOWLEDGEMENTS

Majesty, Honour, and Praise
To God, The Father; Jesus, His Son; and The Holy Spirit

To my Dedicated and Loving Wife
Mary Alice Moody

To my Executive Editor
Rena M. Boston

To my Proofreaders
Le'Trisha Daniel
Rosalyn Dopson
Edward E. Jackson
Naomi Keener
Lisa Laude'-Walker
Cammie Ross

To my Illustrator
Richard Stewart Halstead

Honorable Mention
James Ranger
Faith Temple Family
Barbara Lovett
Tony McClain
Delores Patterson
Mary Webster-Moore

To all of my brothers and sisters in Christ who encouraged me to undergo this project, thank you. To previous writers who attempted this task, I appreciate you. I extend my love to all of my readers. I pray that this book blesses you as God has blessed me.

FOREWORD

Like the prophet Jeremiah, Bishop Carlis Lee Moody, Sr., was called and anointed for God's service while in his mother's womb. His story clearly reflects the truth that God's hand of righteousness protected and preserved him to be a witness of God's grace and a pastor, teacher, and evangelist to Evanston, Illinois and the world.

From his humble beginning in Tifton, Georgia to pastor a great church in Evanston, from the struggles and poverty of a single parent family to the leadership of the Missions Department of a great denomination, from the obscurity of a common laborer at Sears in Chicago to the high office of Bishop, and leadership in the world Pentecostal movement, Bishop Carlis Lee Moody, Sr., has been focused and faithful to God, his family and his church.

Bishop Moody is a successful pastor because he is an obedient anointed servant of God. He loves the Word of God and applies the Word to his life and ministry. His gospel preaching is matched by his practice of holiness and sanctification.

This autobiography reveals the pastor's journey of faith. He acknowledges that his leadership style was shaped by the Word of God, but influenced by seasoned saints, men and women, who touched his life. However, the greatest human influence and most important contributor to his success as a pastor is his beloved wife and companion of more than 50 years. As partners in parenting and ministry they have served as role models for many couples. Their love for each other and their mutual respect have enabled them to experience success and failure, tragedy and triumph while remaining faithful to God.

As a friend of the Moody family since 1976, I have visited their home as well as the Evanston church and have been inspired by their healthy marriage and strong family. The fact that Bishop Moody has shepherded his own household is evident in that all of their children are serving the Lord.

The readers will be inspired by the pastor's faithfulness; whether he is preaching for weeks in an empty tent or holding services in a barber shop. The author speaks frankly about his weaknesses and his dependence on God, who never fails.

I strongly recommend this book. This pastor's testimony will inspire faith and faithfulness. It should be required reading for candidates for ordination in the Church Of God In Christ.

Bishop George D. McKinney,
Pastor and Founder
St. Stephen's Cathedral Church of God in Christ,
San Diego, California

TABLE OF CONTENTS

INTRODUCTION

Give me now wisdom and knowledge, that I may go out and come in before this people...
II Chronicles 1:10a

I marvel at the number of times I have been asked, *"How do you do it?"* From the time and attention I give to children and adults alike, saved and unsaved, to my in-home visits of the saints who are in need, to the hospital visits, to my extensive travels to the foreign field, I cannot say that I understand or can explain 'it' either. We are all amazed at the stamina that God has granted me.

I know that I love the people of God, and it is that love that compels me to do what I do. No matter where I am or who I am with, I may be caught waving at someone I know. It has happened in the middle of the Holy Convocation, on a platform full of dignitaries and in the midst of a formal procession. When I make eye contact with someone I recognize, I just do what comes naturally, sometimes forgetting protocol.

Striving always to be the gentleman and deal with people in a gentle manner, I will often stop what I am doing or change my direction of travel to accommodate someone else. It is just the way God has made me, one who deeply loves people. My desire is that you will come to feel the heart that God has given me for *all* people, and that you will be blessed and encouraged by what you read.

THE MAN

A man is only as much a man as he is walking
in obedience to the Word of God!

A MOTHER'S LOVE

... for her bowels yearned upon her son...
I Kings 3:26a

She was born on July 18, 1916, to Lee and Pearl Wilkerson, and was given the name Geneva. During her lifetime, she married five times, with the first four marriages ending in divorce. Then, in 1956, she married Brother James Smith and her life changed dramatically. Brother Smith preceded her in death, and my mother, Geneva Smith, went home to be with the Lord on July 26, 1996. The years I shared with my mother were filled with love and laughter amidst our struggles to survive.

My maternal grandmother, whom we called Ma'Dear, married when she was about thirteen years of age and gave birth to thirteen children. Before I was born, her husband and five of her children had died. Even though she had eight children to raise, and no longer had a husband to care for her, she never complained. She had very little money, but she did not allow the 'poverty line' mentality to define her. Despair was never one of her companions. During difficult times, she simply called the children to her side and prayed, giving thanks to God, even when nothing was on the table.

While growing up, I periodically lived with my grandmother. At age seven, I traveled alone to visit her. I took the train from Winter Park, Florida to Tifton,

Georgia via Jacksonville. God taught me early in life how to discipline my body for travel. God knew that His plans for my life included travel. My visits with Ma'Dear also provided experiences in manual labor. For fifty cents a day, from sunrise until sunset, we pulled corn, tomatoes, onions and cabbage plants. We also picked up potatoes, cropped tobacco and picked cotton. We were making an honest living.

Some people we knew were sharecroppers; nevertheless, they were still held by poverty's grip. Those who sharecropped were never free of their debt to 'Mr. Charlie,' the name used to refer to the plantation owner. At the end of harvest season, the sharecroppers were advanced money that they were unable to repay during the next season. Somehow, they always came up short.

Those who managed to succeed did so because of their wives. I lived with my Uncle Robert and Aunt Marie at one time, and I watched my aunt help my uncle. As often as she could, Aunt Marie would save a few dollars so that when the time came to settle the account, she could help her husband. Their account was paid-in-full.

Like the Apostle Paul, I learned contentment in many situations. During later years, even after getting electricity, we did not have a bathroom. We had an outhouse and took baths in a number two tin tub. We carried our bath water from the creek. To heat the water, Ma'Dear would place the smoothing iron in the fire, and after it was heated, she placed it in the tub of water. We used soap that was made of lye and lard.

Since we could not afford to buy food from the store, we planted gardens. Glass jars were used to preserve food for the winter. Ma'Dear also raised chickens. When I was small, Ma'Dear did not have a stove. Instead, she laid two bricks in the yard, placed an old stove rack across them, built a fire, and cooked our food. The emptied flour sacks were washed and used to make ladies' dresses and undergarments. Ma'Dear never complained, and for me, it was just a way of life. My grandmother lived to be eighty-four, and she taught me not to worry. Her philosophy was simply, *"Deal with every situation as best as you can."*

I learned a lot while living with my grandmother, and I saw the faithfulness of God to His Word and to her. Ma'Dear had suffered from asthma for fifty years, and periodically had sleepless nights. To help her rest better, we propped her up in bed, saturated some cotton with sulfur and burnt it. The fumes opened her lungs, allowing her to breathe easier. One day, miraculously, Jesus reached down and touched her body and made her whole. I witnessed God heal my grandmother.

I also remember my great grandmother Mary. She had been born into slavery, and had not learned to read until God saved her and filled her with the Holy Ghost. The Holy Ghost taught her how to read the Bible. She often laid her hands on me and asked God to bless my life. I remember hearing her, late into the night, speaking in some strange language. I did not understand that she was speaking in tongues, but I knew that to whomever she was talking, she loved Him. Later, I realized that she was talking to Jesus.

My mother was the love of my heart, and the Lord gave her continual grace. Although she only had an eighth grade education, she had good common sense, 'mother wit'. When she committed her life to the Lord, He gave her godly wisdom. However, there was a time, before she knew the Lord, when mama made some bad decisions. She home-brewed whiskey and her sampling of the merchandise turned into drinking. Bad things began to happen. My mother's younger sister started drinking whiskey also. They became a team and often shared the same bottle. They would sneak whiskey into their bedroom and sip it during the night.

One evening, one of them forgot to place the cap back on the bottle. Our house was located near a peanut plant that was infested with gigantic roaches. These were the biggest roaches I had ever seen! While my mother and her sister slept, one of the roaches crawled into the open bottle. Sipping time came again. My aunt took a sip and gave the bottle to my mother. When Mama picked up the bottle and placed it to her mouth, she saw the roach leaping in the bottom of the bottle. That was the end of Mama's drinking habit. She was unsaved, but she said, *"No more"*, and from that night on, she never had another drink.

During my mother's early years, she had a quick temper, which usually lay dormant unless she was provoked. She was also a marksman with a knife and an ice pick. What she did not do with the knife, she could left-handedly do with the ice pick. Mama was so tough that if she needed to discipline us while she was cooking, she would spank us with a knife on our rear ends, never once cutting us.

Mama was a shapely and attractive woman. She gave young men who showed interest in her, one warning. She told them, *"We are gonna make it, as long as you don't put your hands on me to abuse me. If you do, then we've got trouble. My mother has already raised me, and if you think you've got to raise me again, then you'd better let me go home"*. I never had to worry about my mother not being able to defend herself.

As a child, I was secure in my mother's love. When the natural love of my mother could go no further, the love of God made up the difference. The Bible says, when father and mother forsake you, the Lord will take you up. We are called to live in the assurance that God will never leave us nor forsake us. I had to accept this truth at an early age.

I was the biological son of Mr. Booker T. Moody. I was born on December 16, 1934. When I was three years of age, my daddy left us without a word. Shortly thereafter, he returned. At the age of five, he left again. My mother remarried between the departures and returns. At the age of seven, I stood with my mother at the train station and watched my father leave again. This time he was leaving to find work in Rochester, New York. He found employment as a chauffeur, but he never came home again. In his lifetime, he remarried three times after my mother. Every year my dad would call me on my birthday and Christmas. He never sent money or a gift, but he called. I received what fatherly nurturing he could give through his annual telephone calls. This was my plight for more than twelve years of my youth.

As a young boy, I became the stepson of four men and had a total of eleven step sisters and brothers. I had many daddies and yet, I had none. I had one Father, whose name is God. All of the men that my mother married said good-bye and were gone, until my mother married Brother James Smith. He became a loving father to me. He was very instrumental in my life, but it was God who taught me and met me at the point of my deepest need.

A lot has been said about single-parenting and latch-key children. More negatives have been expressed than positives, and more failures cited than successes touted. Some people look at me now and think I had an easy life, but that couldn't be further from the truth. I was an only child for twenty-two years. For much of that time, my mother was my only parent, and God was my only God. As I grew from a teen to a young adult, our life became a living testimony against society's indictments concerning single-parenting and latch-key children.

During my teen years we moved further north. We lived in Waukegan, Illinois while my mother worked twenty miles away in Winnetka, Illinois. My mother stayed in the home of her employers from Friday to Wednesday, and came home every other Thursday and every Sunday. However, if her employers left town for a month, she would not come home at all during that month. Instead, she would have someone stop by our house and check on me. I always made sure that things were in order. From age fifteen to twenty, I did most of the cleaning, cooking, and ironing.

My mother rested in the confidence that God loved her son and her son loved God. She knew that she could leave me home alone and I would be alright. I recognized that my mother's work decision was for our survival and not neglect. I was a sensitive and tender child who loved my mother very much. I did whatever I could to lessen her burden. It grieved my heart to see my mother work so hard to earn a living. She earned approximately $25-$35 a week. I purposed in my heart that when I became of age, I would drop out of school, get a job, and help my mother. Times were pretty hard and I wanted to be there for her. We were in the struggle together and we needed each other.

My mother promised that she would take care of me as best she could. She told me, *"Anything I don't get you is either because I can't afford it, or because you don't need it."* I rarely knew which reason applied because it was a settled issue. My mother never told me I was poor. She just said, *"We are making an honest living."* Her honesty enabled me to dispel feelings of self-pity and low self-esteem. I learned contentment with a grateful heart.

For example, I wore white shirts practically all of my life because my mother was able to purchase them by the bulk from the Salvation Army. Each shirt cost ten cents. And even in that situation, I didn't view us as poor. My mother was a source of strength and power.

At fifteen, I landed my first job as a day laborer for the Amoco Tools Steel Factory. When that job ended, I accepted a position with the Woolworth Department Store. I cleaned the offices at night after closing. Later I worked in the homes of the wealthy; homes located in Highland Park, Kenilworth and Winnetka. I washed windows, mopped floors, cleaned garages, and did whatever else I could to help my mother earn a living.

Although my mom's job often kept her away from home, she called periodically to assure herself that I was well and my needs were met. Because of my love for and involvement in the church, she could locate me anytime, day or night. I would either be at home, school, church, or with a church family. Sometimes her call wasn't to locate me but to reach me. She would call when she sensed in her spirit that something was wrong. Those were love calls that gave me an opportunity to address a specific need in my life. When I answered the telephone, she simply said, *"Carlis, what's wrong?"* I would pour out my heart about everything that was bothering me. I found comfort in my mother's love. It reached me wherever I was and whenever I was hurting.

As close as my mother and I were, she never tolerated

disrespect. There were rules governing our relationship. I could talk to her about anything and while I explained, she listened. She never, however, allowed me to have the last word, nor did I speak while she was talking. I learned at an early age how to hold my thoughts. I never lied to mama about anything because I was too afraid. If there was something difficult that I needed to tell her, I would try to determine how angry it would make her before telling her. Regardless of her reaction, I knew that sooner or later, I had to face her. Usually it was easier than I expected. We were bonded together in more ways than I had realized.

Today, I thank God that this latch-key kid of a single parent never became one of the negative statistics that society touts. Although I dropped out of high school for a year to work and help my mother, I returned, attended school half days, and continued to work. I studied long and hard, taking history courses through the University of Nebraska. God blessed me to complete my studies, get all of my credits, and graduate from high school in three years and eight weeks.

At age eighteen, I journeyed to New York City to visit my father. I met my father's wife, visited for a short while, and returned home. Ten years later, I packed up my family and headed for New York City again. This time it was for my father and my family to meet each other. After that visit, I only saw my father two more times prior to his death. Although I accomplished my goal of getting reacquainted and settling some unanswered questions, I found that the lost years could not be recovered. In 1978, at age sixty-four, Mr. Booker T. died of a heart attack. To my knowledge, he never accepted Jesus as his personal Saviour.

AN INSTRUMENT IN THE HAND OF GOD

Train up a child in the way he should go:
and when he is old, he will not depart from it.
Proverbs 22:6

We are instruments in the hand of God. Just as God molds our lives, we are responsible for molding the lives of those whom He has entrusted in our care. I firmly believe that a musical instrument should be placed in the hands of every child, until the gift of God within them is manifested. You may discover that the child has a natural ability to skillfully play that instrument. I also believe that every child should learn a second language. We should encourage our children to be and do their best. Our encouragement helps remove the fears and limitations they may encounter. This is yet another means by which we expand their lives. Parents' expectations should exceed what a child currently does.

God gave me the ability to play the piano, organ, guitar, and saxophone. If I had never touched these instruments, I would not have known that I was anointed to play. God had already given me an ear for music. It was so natural for me. Even with unfamiliar instruments and music, I comfortably and confidently played. My skills on each instrument were self-developed, with the exception of some basic piano concepts taught to me by Bishop Nick Hightower.

Ma'Dear had an upright piano at the foot of her bed and I never hesitated to practice or play on it. Soon I had mastered the piano, and moved on to other musical instruments available to me. When we put forth an effort to learn, God is faithful to stir up and perfect the gifts that are within us.

When we moved North, I joined the high school band. My instrument of choice was the saxophone. I played all four years even though I could not read one musical note. The Holy Spirit knew the notes, and I just trusted Jesus for that area of knowledge. It was a challenge learning to play different instruments, but the saints were always there to encourage me. When I made a mistake, they simply said, *"Bless him, Lord."* And that's exactly what God did; He blessed me! Today, I can skillfully play all four instruments, and I still do not read music.

After God had perfected those gifts within me, I was offered a contract to play the blues with David Rockingham. David told me that I could make some big money. He also said that I would be free to preach on Sunday mornings. This did not align with the Word of God, so I declined the offer. I wanted to give back to God the gifts He gave to me. He had entrusted me with a talent and I wanted that talent to praise Him. The instruments in my hands belonged to God alone.

There is another gift that has been with me since early childhood. It came through my grandmother's improvisation in our home life, and led to a life-changing experience for me. To decorate our home *and* keep me entertained, Ma'Dear covered the walls and ceilings with pages of old Sunday school scrolls. Whether I was awake, preparing for bed, or just relaxing, I was surrounded by the Word of God. I read the Word day and night and memorized the scriptures.

To this day, the saints of Faith Temple often marvel at my ability to recite the scriptures. When a minister begins to read the scripture references for my sermons, he often struggles to keep up with me because I recite the verses faster than he can read them. I want to encourage you just as the prophet Zechariah did when he said to not despise the day of small things, since we never know what bigger and better things God has planned for us.

In the church I attended as a child, the preacher prayed for people during worship services. Those who came to the altar to be saved would receive prayer until they were saved. However, when I went to the altar, the altar workers would send me back to my seat because I was a child. I returned to my seat crying. I did not understand why they did not want to spend time with me. The last time this happened I said, *"I'm going to live with my grandmother and I'm going to get saved there!"*

That's just what I did.

One of the reasons I wanted to get saved was because I had heard a preacher preach about hell-fire. As the sermon went forth, I began to experience such a similitude of hell fire that my pants felt hot. I thought if hell was *that* hot, I had better get things straight with God. I already knew that God loved me, but I needed to surrender my life to Him. I did not know anything about praying the sinner's prayer. All I knew to do was cry out, *"Lord, save me!"* and when I said that, He did. I did not need my grandmother or mother to confirm the fact that I was saved. I knew it for myself.

Although I was saved at a young age, I still played and got into things like other children. I remember the first time I tried to skate. I placed the skates on my feet and slide right under a car. I got up, took the skates off, and never put them on again. There were other times when my cousins and I designed and tested our own toys. We used pine tree branches to make a swing. Interesting enough, I was always the guinea pig. After a few tosses back and forth, I got so dizzy that I retired as the family toy tester.

My cousin and I found amusement in teasing animals. One day we were antagonizing a helpless cat. Suddenly, my cousin left the room, slammed the door, and locked it, leaving me alone with the angry cat. I was scared. While carefully watching me, the cat jumped on the mantle and bristled. It was no longer the cat's turn to run; it was mine. As the cat seemed to grow before my very eyes, I started banging on the door and yelling, *"Let me out!"* After a while, the cat calmed down realizing that I would not harm him. Finally, my cousin returned to let me out. The cat jumped off the mantle and beat me out the door.

Sometimes Aunt Bessie Mae would have to babysit me. When she had other plans, she would give me money and send me to the movies. One movie cost nine cents while the other cost thirteen cents. With a quarter, I could spend an entire day watching one movie after another. I enjoyed my day at the movies. Years later, we watched in-home movies on television, but the saints told me, *"Son, you can't watch television"*. I did not understand, nevertheless I obeyed.

I was a young child with strong convictions about my faith. I was not easily swayed from my teachings and beliefs. I had no problem telling people that I was saved. I did not care what others thought about my being saved. When some of the children asked, *"Why do you go to church all of the time?"* My answer was always, *"Because I want to."* I rarely missed a service. I was committed to serve God to the end. From the day of my salvation (at age nine) to now, I have never thought about, considered or desired to turn back from following the Lord.

One day a big guy picked me up and held me by my heels to scare me into changing my conviction. He shook me until everything fell out of my pockets. When he placed me back on the ground, I held to my conviction. At that moment I knew that you have to be bold for God. Life experiences were not the only contributing factors in my determination to walk with the Lord. Observing the wisdom of God in the saints' lives had a significant impact.

The saints taught me how to have a fruitful relationship with God. You had to study the word of God, fast, and pray. I purposed in my heart that I wanted to stand firm in God. I wanted a consistent and a fortified walk with the Lord, so I did what was suggested. I fasted the first three days of each month and on Tuesday and Friday of each week. I prayed and studied the word of God every day.

Ma'Dear studied the Word of God with me. Without a television to distract us, we studied often. Each week we would review the Sunday school lessons together. Our church revivals lasted a minimum of one month. I would attend every service I possibly could. The more I was taught about God, the more I wanted to know about Him.

After being saved, I learned that a lot of things were considered a 'no-no.' You were expected to live holy, without sin. The saints believed that if you had a bad habit like drinking, smoking or adultery, you stayed on the altar in the Lord's presence until whatever was hanging on, dropped off. The saints knew that God could free you from the bondage of sin.

At an early age, I learned that every one of us was subject to failure. The only way to ensure success is to totally lean on Jesus. No matter what you have overcome in the past, the person who 'used to do' certain things will do them again unless they receive continual help from God. As I have matured in life and the Lord, my reputation has become that of a humble, respectable servant of God and a scholar of the Bible who loves God and His people. It is my prayer that God will testify of my purity, righteousness and holiness, when He comes to take me home.

At the age of ten, in Tifton, Georgia, I was bedridden with a fever of 105°. My loving grandmother stood, sat and slept by my side. For two weeks I battled this sickness. My listless body was parched so badly that my skin began to peel. The fever destroyed the soles of my feet, which made it difficult to walk. I had prayed and my grandmother had done all that was humanly possible to do. I laid there waiting on God and His will for my life. Fortunately, I had learned much earlier that my life was in God's hands.

At this critical moment in my life, the Holy Ghost led an unknown servant of God to me. The man of God said that he was told by the Holy Spirit to go and pray for a sick boy. The man did not know the location, but being led of the Holy Ghost, he knocked on our door. Ma'Dear answered and he asked, *"Is there a sick boy here?"* My grandmother said, *"Yes."* He explained his commission and my grandmother invited him in. The man of God prayed and left. Immediately, I rose from the bed of affliction. However, when the fever broke, it left me extremely weak, requiring crutches to walk.

My life and love for God, since the tender age of nine, caused the saints to fast, pray and petition God for help in my time of trouble. On Tuesday, the church proclaimed a shut-in to fast and pray for my complete healing. The brethren came together in unity of heart and purpose, determined that they would not leave until they heard from God.

I was laid on a pallet where I remained during the fasting and prayer. Suddenly, the power and presence of God came upon me and caused me to leap up. When I leaped up, I began to dance before the Lord. I have been dancing and shouting the victory ever since. Sickness is often feared by many and unwelcomed by all. We must realize that even in sickness we are victorious if we trust God for our deliverance.

PREACHER BOY

...if He call thee, that thou shalt say,
Speak, Lord; for thy servant heareth.
I Samuel 3:9a

My commitment to serve God brought challenges, many of which came in the early days after my call to preach. Approximately six months prior to my call however, my pastor 'silenced' me. He sent me on an errand and told me to come straight back. On the way, I saw another brother going a different direction. He asked me to wait for him so that we could go back to the church together. I agreed to wait for him instead of obeying my pastor's instructions.

This was the first and only time that I had disobeyed my pastor. My record of loyalty and obedience did not earn me any mercy from him. My pastor asked me, *"Should I whip you or silence you?"* Since I loved to dance in the worship services I opted to be whipped rather than silenced. Naturally, he chose to do the opposite. Being silenced meant sitting alone on the back pew and not participating in the service, which included dancing, singing and testifying. Each Sunday I could move up one row. Finally, when I reached the first row, I was sent to the altar.

I decided that if a leader told me to do something, even if I disagreed, I would do it as long as it was not something against the word of God. I learned to obey from my pastor's literal application of the Apostle Paul's admonition to young Timothy: *"Them that sin, rebuke before all that others may also fear."* This was one of the greatest lessons I was ever taught, the lesson of respect for authority. I did not know that within months I would be in a position of authority myself, but *God* knew.

I was called to preach on July 26, 1946, at the age of eleven years old. There is one voice, which will not be ignored and that is the voice of God. When God called me to the ministry, I responded, *"No, not me!"* God replied, *"Yes, you!"* Knowing that I heard from the Lord, I informed my pastor, who instructed me to pray. In obedience, I consecrated myself for three days. I prayed that God would confirm His call by saving one soul during my first sermon. I had no idea when the opportunity to preach would come, but I was committed to the call and ready to answer it.

Through divine intervention, the opportunity arrived. I was asked to preach at a worship service because no other preacher was present. My sermon, taken from the sixth chapter of Genesis, was entitled 'It's Gonna Rain.' God gave me confirmation. Exactly one soul was saved during the service.

The Apostle Paul tells of his perils in life, but I experienced my own. What does an eleven year old know about suffering? I was called to preach while my school teacher was called to teach *and* beat. I preached because I was called, and I was beaten because I preached. It did not seem right, but I realized that God was preparing me for something. I recognized that evil devices and people could be instruments to accomplish God's plan.

When I prepared for school, my Bible was as important as the textbooks. It was my life, the only life I knew. I loved to read my Bible and preach to the children during recess. Mrs. Williams, however, decided that this was not proper behavior for school. She forbade me to read my Bible during recess or to preach to the children. Needless to say, we did not see eye-to-eye. I refused to obey her because the other children were allowed to read comic books. If they could read their comic books during recess, then I should be allowed to read my Bible. The only difference was our choice in a Super Hero. Hence, I continued to read and preach the Gospel. Repeatedly, I was beaten for doing so. Despite the beatings, I returned to school each day more determined than the day before. I knew the word of God was true, and believed I should live by it. No price was too high. I was both aggressive and stubborn, but God can take our negative characteristics and sanctify them for His glory. I continued on as before. This only increased the teacher's agitation which in turn increased her punishments. She did not allow me to go outside during recess. I was persistent and determined. While I sat alone in the classroom, I opened the windows, stood on a stool and preached to the children on the playground.

The teacher decided that my actions warranted a higher degree of punishment so she beat me in the palm of my hands with a piece of rubber from the fan belt of a car. The beatings left my hands bruised and swollen. I never told my mother or grandmother. I feared what my grandmother would do to the teacher. I told Uncle Richard because the swelling of my hands prevented me from completing my chores. Uncle Richard did my chores until my hands healed. I continued reading my Bible and preaching and the beatings continued. To some of my classmates, the life of this eleven-year-old boy preacher did not seem too delightful, but I rejoiced because I was committed to the call. I consistently hid the scars and swelling from mama and Ma'Dear. Ma'Dear and I were very close; I loved her, but I also knew her tolerance level and the extent of her anger. So I kept silent before her. God strengthened me, and I endured the harshness.

Keeping the beatings a secret was perhaps, my way of forgiving and protecting the teacher who continually beat me. Years later our paths crossed again. I returned to Tifton, Georgia to visit my grandmother. While I was there, I visited Mrs. Williams. As we talked, she proclaimed that her eyes had been opened and she had received the Lord Jesus Christ as her personal Saviour. The teacher of 'beatings' looked into my eyes and said, *"I now understand what you were saying and doing."* At that moment, she confirmed what I already knew, "every lash was worth it all, and I could indeed count it all joy!"

My childhood trials continued. In 1948, now thirteen years old, I preached at a service in Lake City, Florida. The saints gave me an offering. Later that night as I slept at my pastor's home, someone entered my room and stole my money. A family friend, Thomas, was also staying there. I felt like he had taken my money. I was hurt, angry and a long way from home. I decided to take action although it was never proven that Thomas had actually stolen the money. I knew my pastor owned a 38-caliber pistol. I decided to borrow it to help settle the score with my friend. Thomas was much taller and stronger than me, but the pistol would balance the scale.

Before doing anything foolish, God intervened. In my young mind I thought, *"If I kill him, he won't live to forgive me for doing so."* I decided against retaliation of any kind. I repented to Thomas and God for what I had planned.

In 1948, I was again called to Florida to preach. This time I was scheduled to conduct a revival in Jacksonville at Elder Ralph Ragland's church. On the way there I was robbed in the train station. I placed my wallet on the counter to write a telegram. A man, pretending to be crippled, walked towards me, took it and left hastily. I was left with nothing. I began walking to the church. Finally a man who recognized me offered me a ride. When he asked why I was walking, I immediately burst into tears. One thing is certain, I learned valuable lessons from these experiences which enabled me to implement a new way of securing my money. I began tying my money in the tail of my shirt to keep it close to me.

Serving God in your youth does not change your childish tendencies, but rather prepares you for your future as an adult.

Obedience is indeed better than sacrifice, even for a boy preacher on a mission for God. On one occasion, my mother forced me to go with my stepfather to preach in Sanford, Florida. Despite my strong opposition, I went. My stepfather was lazy and refused to work. I was angry about the possibility that he might benefit from my preaching.

We arrived in Sanford on Tuesday. On Wednesday, I decided to run away. I left my stepfather in Sanford and went to Lake City, Florida, where I preached alone. For five days none of my relatives knew where I was. During my absence, God's hand of protection covered me. On the following Monday, I returned home and my mother showed me mercy.

Even though I obtained mercy, God's word remains true. He expects our obedience. We cannot afford to frustrate the grace of God.

In 1949, my stepfather left my mother and me for a new, separate life. I'm sure that it probably made my mother sad, but I had no regrets. Mom and I just moved forward with our lives. In 1950, we moved to Illinois.

The wrath of man worketh not the righteousness of God; but if we are patient, God works all things out for our good. When we trust God, He will never fail us. When the Lord called me, He promised to take good care of my mother and me. God has always kept His word.

Even when people tried to misuse us, God always intervened. My mother and I moved from Tifton, Georgia to Waukegan, Illinois to help build the music ministry for an Elder's church. Since I played the piano, I agreed to come and use my gift to help him. My services were without charge. Shortly after our arrival, he began taking advantage of us. He provided us a place to sleep in his living room and charged us $19 a week for rent. He knew, we knew and, more importantly, God knew that this was not right. We left the situation in God's hand. God blessed the little that mom had left and enabled her to take care of our personal needs.

One day the elder with whom we were staying seemed to lose his mind. He badly beat his wife and daughter. The police were called and he was arrested. The preacher messed up so terribly that his members did not know where to go or what to do. The church was in an upheaval. There I was, a fifteen-year-old boy, about to inherit a church. I was appointed pastor in the preacher's stead. Needless to say, at age fifteen, I did not know how to pastor or lead a congregation. However, I had the Holy Ghost and loved God and His people. God allowed me to pastor those saints for a while. Afterwards, the Lord led me to a seasoned pastor who was a good shepherd for us all.

I was ordained at age sixteen. However, I have since learned that preachers should practice what they've learned before ordination. The person in ministry is much like the person studying to become a doctor. An aspiring doctor goes to school to learn the principles of the trade. After successful completion of school, one enters an internship to practice what he or she has learned. Preachers who desire to pastor must learn 'the discipline of leadership'. In order to effectively lead, they must learn to explicitly follow leadership. First and foremost, they must follow Christ; secondly, since many religious organizations are hierarchically structured, they must follow the rules of their church organization. Following leadership not only reveals how to be obedient and submissive to authority, but also provides insight into what a leader must consider.

A good preacher is stirred to talk with people, and oftentimes doesn't call it preaching. When God called me, He placed preaching in my bones. It was as if every one of my conversations became a sermon. The knowledge of life and the suddenness and certainty of death cause me to warn people, through preaching the gospel. I preach and preach, sometimes preaching until it hurts inside. I preach so hard because I see people that are in the church and still on their way to hell. They sit as if nothing is happening, and I know that if they should suddenly die, they would be lost.

Nevertheless, I persevere and preach God's word with the certainty of standing before God and hearing Him say, *"Well done, good and faithful servant."*

With the confirmation of my call came the onslaught of challenges within and outside the church. When I preached in our local assembly, one of the mothers was there to give her words of 'encouragement'. In the heat of my sermon, when I was preaching well, that mother's voice would ring out with, *"You need to sit down!"* This did not happen once or twice, nor was it the result of a bad day. This was a concerted effort to consistently discourage me.

I was seriously wounded by her numerous outbursts. They pierced so deeply because they were said loud enough for the entire church to hear. Yet I had to continue as if nothing had happened. Once, my feelings were hurt so badly that I ran home to mama, fell across the bed and cried. Through the pain, I yelled, *"I'm not going back there anymore!"* When my tears ceased, I realized that my hurt feelings departed with the tears.

Later, I realized that the mother loved me deeply. That was her way of aiding in my spiritual development. She knew what I did not: the years ahead would bring its' own barrages of discouragement. I concluded that any saint who could withstand the offenses of the brethren was surely on his or her way to heaven. I learned what it meant to 'endure hardness as a good soldier of Jesus Christ'.

THAT GIRL

Who can find a virtuous woman?
For her price is far above rubies.
Proverbs 31:10

Years ago, girls were married as early as age thirteen. The young man took his wife home to his parents, and his parents would finish raising the both of them. Young couples then had some of the same disagreements as young couples today. Back then, however, there was always a referee. Although the referees were not perfect, their intervention helped establish a strong foundation for young marriages.

In today's society, people marry much later. The

longer they wait, the more demands they place on each other. Marriages today often begin with many expectations, some of which are realistic and others unrealistic. Everyone is looking for stability. Perhaps the advantage of marrying early is that the couple does not yet know what to expect of each other.

I first met my wife at the home of one of my mother's closest friends, Mrs. Anna Bertha Gipson. We were living in North Chicago and our house was about four doors from Mrs. Anna Bertha's house, where I went each day after school. The first time I saw Mary, the Lord spoke to me and said, *"That girl is going to be your wife."* I did not know her name, so I went to the kitchen where Mrs. Anna Bertha was and asked about her. I needed to know something about the girl whom God had chosen for me. She was very attractive with thick, dark hair, rich chocolate skin and a beautiful smile. I learned that her name was Mary Alice Byrd and she was not saved. Now that was a problem because I had previously told the Lord that I would not talk to any girl unless she was saved and this young lady, though attractive, was no exception. I did not compromise my position, but I did wait because I knew that she was worth waiting for.

A few months later, she committed her life to the Lord. I talked to the Lord again and told Him that I still would not date her until she received the baptism of the Holy Ghost. Months later, she was filled with the Holy Ghost. Then I asked her to be my girlfriend, and she consented.

I visited her every Thursday night and telephoned her every Friday night. When I first started going to her house, my visits were with the entire family. Everyone was present, including her four sisters and four brothers. The world's concept of dating is vastly different from that of the saints. In the world, you may date for five years, get married, and get a divorce six months later. If a saint desires to get married, they should pray and then wait until God sends them their mate. Our trouble comes when God does not hurry and we take matters into our own hands.

Usually when I visited Mary, I was so tired that I would fall asleep while talking. If the room was cool, she would spread a blanket over me and let me sleep while she did whatever she had to do. When it was time for me to leave, she shook me and said, *"Elder Moody, it's time to go home."* We did not routinely spend time alone; however, after I asked her to be my girlfriend, I had the privilege of sitting in the Living Room alone with her on Thursday evenings. And on another occasion, we were alone when we went to the store for her mom. Otherwise, someone always accompanied us. Of course, I had no problem with that because it was in line with my principles of dating.

According to the scripture, saints greeted each other with a holy kiss. However, young girls and boys did not embrace each other. Some other basic teachings I received were these:

- Every male and female born into the world

becomes sexually alive when they reach a certain age.

- If you play with fire, you are going to get burned.
- If you engage in sex before marriage, even if you don't get the girl pregnant, you leave a part of you with her. When you get married, problems could develop because of the tendency to compare your mate with your prior partners.
- A young man who goes from one woman to another, even if he does not get married, will never know how to treat women with respect.

We should train our boys to know that God holds them responsible for the children they father. They should not have babies here and there because they cannot possibly fulfill the responsibilities of multiple households.

When I talked with Mary, I only spoke about things pertaining to our future together. I told her what I wanted in a wife and what I had to offer a wife. As we continued to talk, we became better acquainted. Our communication helped us to know each other very well.

One of the most beautiful love stories I recall was that of my friends Carol Ann and Richard Daye. Their love was made in heaven and manifested on earth. And love, when done right, produces great and lasting results. Carol Ann was a dear friend I met when my mother and I moved to North Chicago. Her mother assisted us in finding a house to rent. She and her mom became our closest family. Carol and I attended

Waukegan Township High School. While Carol Ann was still in high school, a friend showed her picture to a Navy man named Richard Daye. When Richard saw the picture, he said, *"That girl is going to be my wife."* Shortly after seeing the picture, Richard's friend arranged for them to meet. When Richard expressed his desire to marry her, she never disagreed.

When Richard received military leave, he met her parents and told them of his intentions to marry their daughter. Her parents told him that she was too young for marriage, and that she was still in school. He responded, *"I'll wait."* He returned to Seattle, where he was stationed and finished his tour of duty. After receiving his discharge, he went back home to visit his mother and wait for his wife-to-be. When Carol Ann graduated from high school, he returned to her parents' home to receive his wife. Carol Ann and Richard got married and for a lifetime, they lived a very happy life together, until the Lord called Carol Ann home.

Now I was at the same crossroad as Richard. I wanted Mary as my wife, but I did not have a job. Mary's father clearly told me that I could not marry his daughter without a job. So I began my search for a job. I searched every day because I wanted to marry Mary. I walked from place to place, filling out applications everywhere I could. I was extremely tired, but I prayed and kept going.

One day I sat on the sidewalk and spoke these simple words, *"Jesus, I need a job."* Jesus heard and He answered. Elder S.M. Ward, pastor of Ward Memorial Church of God in Christ, in Waukegan, Illinois, came to me and offered to take me to Sears to apply for a job. The Sears representative told Elder Ward that he did not have a job for me. While sitting there waiting, I prayed, *"Lord, I need a job."* Shortly after I finished praying, the same man who said he did not have a job, *created* one for me. My duties included changing the light bulbs and cleaning the light fixtures throughout the store. My diligence in performing those duties caused the same man to give me additional responsibilities, which included counting the cars that came into the parking lot. Again, my committed work ethics resulted in a promotion to the automotive department, where I tailored and installed car seat covers. I worked there until God called me into the ministry full time. I have continued to work with diligence, only now, it is in the harvest fields of the Lord. Praise be to God for the lessons of life which often help to prepare us for a life of ministry.

Finally the much anticipated day, September 3, 1955, came when Mary Alice Byrd and I were married. I was twenty years old and Mary was seventeen. She was born December 22, 1937. I was so happy to know that she was willing to marry me even though we had never really dated, hugged, or kissed. As a matter of fact, I never even told her that I loved her. During the wedding ceremony, as the preacher read the vows, I touched her and asked, *"Do you understand what the preacher is saying?"*

I had made a firm decision that if she did not understand what she was doing, we would stop the wedding. She answered, *"Yes,"* and we continued with the ceremony. I was committed to my marriage and to becoming the best husband I could be, so I told her, *"If I don't treat you right, you may tell the church, and I will do likewise if you don't treat me right."* We had a very humble beginning. On our wedding night, there was no elaborate dinner. I could only afford to buy one hamburger for us to share.

As much as I was committed to making our marriage work, we still needed a lot of help. We were married on Saturday and I left my new wife to attend our church's district meeting on Monday night. Our wedding was in September and the Holy Convocation was November, in Memphis. Again, I left my new wife to go to the Convocation. My young bride would throw tantrums and lock herself in the bathroom, crying hysterically. I would beg her to come out, but she would refuse. Sister Lillie Anderson, our landlady, would persuade her to come out. When Sister Anderson ministered to us, I listened, even when it hurt. It was good to have someone to counsel us.

I loved my wife. God taught me that we must love and trust Him and each other during times of trouble. Only then would we live victorious lives and enjoy a successful marriage. I called my wife 'Baby' as soon as we were married and 50 years later, her name is still 'Baby'.

Getting married so young and not knowing the facts

of life, we had some real problems. God had to give me wisdom to be a husband and father since no one taught me in word or deed. There were things my mother felt uncomfortable teaching me. My daddy was not around, so she placed me in the hands of the preacher. This did not help my situation. The preacher was unaware that *I* did not know what to do or *how* to do it. So he just shared general information about marriage.

The preacher talked about everything except what I needed to know, and no one else told me anything. All I knew was one day I would marry, have sex with my wife, and have babies. Consequently, when I got married, I was as inexperienced as they come. We did not know much about marriage counselors but we found one quickly. My wife poured out her heart to him first. Then I had the opportunity to do the same. During and after counseling, I prayed and told the Lord that I wanted to be married to this girl for the rest of my life. The counselor gave us some helpful pointers. We went home, discussed them, and practiced them. From then on, it was smooth sailing.

Exactly nine months and three days from our wedding date, our first child was born. Approximately one year and two weeks later, our second child arrived. By the time I was twenty-six we had four children. Our friends began mocking us. They repeatedly criticized us for having so many babies. They said that I was doing what so many preachers do, have baby-after-baby. We didn't concern ourselves with what people said. However, I made it my business to ensure that whatever people said, did not come true. During my wife's pregnancies, I laid my hands on her stomach and prayed for each child. When it was time for our first child, Sideary, to be born, my wife was very small and could barely endure the pain. Of course, I was there to hold her hand. She squeezed my hands so tightly that they were numb. With God's help, we made it successfully through this and three more pregnancies.

All of our children were born healthy. However, when Carlis Jr., our first son, was a year old, we noticed that tears continually ran from his eyes. We decided to have him examined. Our family doctor determined that Carlis Jr. would need surgery because his tear ducts were closed. We decided to believe God. We did not agree to the surgery or consider the doctor's word as final.

When we returned home, we placed Carlis Jr. in the middle of the bed and prayed. My wife stood on one side and I on the other. I'm not sure how long we prayed, but Carlis Jr. sat up in bed with open tear ducts. The devil did not give up. Later, at age eight, Carlis Jr. began suffering with hay fever. We dreaded summer's arrival, because his entire face would swell. Again, we went to the Lord in prayer, and He healed him.

Our life was rapidly progressing, and so were our responsibilities. The time came when I had to help with housework. I was a great help taking clothes to the laundromat, but I did not know how to economically shop for groceries. While growing up in the south, we shopped at the "grab-all" store. This was a store where the storeowner grabbed all of your money and kept your grocery record in a book under the counter. It was amazing that no matter how much money the owner grabbed, our record was never 'paid-in-full.' Grocery shopping was one of the many things my wife taught me early in our marriage.

As time passed and the family grew, finances became scarce. I lived in North Chicago and pastored a church in Evanston. In order to purchase gas to get home, I would pawn a silver dollar. When I had gas money I would reclaim the silver dollar. This cycle repeated many times. Through all of our struggles, my wife supported me and never complained. For that, I love her, the more.

Baby taught me how to save money. Once we saved $800 in dimes which financed our first vacation. We couldn't afford expensive family trips so we took the children to Wisconsin Dells. We selected rides where you paid once and rode repeatedly. We also took little nature trips and picked berries. These low-cost vacations gave us time together as a family and enabled us to progress financially.

The church was also a blessing. We did not have much money for food. Therefore, each Friday night a basket was placed in the corner of the church for a food collection called 'pounds'. Each saint brought a pound of food for the basket. The Lord faithfully fed us through His people. To further assist us, Brother John and Sister Lillie (Sugar) Anderson, who had no children of their own, became Sideary's godparents. They bought her clothes for the first five years of her life. Carlis Jr's godfather, Willie Ridley, would also buy *his* clothes for special occasions.

Our first home in Evanston was a rental from the son of one of the Mothers of the church. It was located on Florence Avenue. The kids were not allowed to play in the yard. In our second home, located on Simpson Street, we did not have a yard for the kids to play in. My wife would take them to the park. Desiring to maintain an active role in their lives, I came home from work during my lunch break to take them to the park. I took fifty minutes to eat my peanut butter and jelly sandwich, play and swing with the children, and return to work on time. I was learning how to be a father, and God and Baby were teaching me.

Watching our children grow reminded me of what the saints told me when I was young. They said that parents helped Jesus to save their children. Therefore *we* had to develop a plan to help Jesus save *our* children. My wife and I always had our own devotion time. Later in our marriage, we joined together to seek the Lord. Baby was the first to recognize the need for us to come together as a family and pray daily with our children. Before I left for work and the children for school, I prayed with them every single day. When I was away, my wife prayed. Family devotions taught our children how to pray.

Teaching our children the Word of God is critical whether they understand or agree with it. In my early years, I had a pastor who could not read, yet we spent all day studying the Word of God. As I read to him, he received revelation from God. Very few people knew he could not read, because it was not apparent when he preached. Our spirits were so fitly joined that as he preached, I knew what scripture he wanted next. I would turn to that passage and read it aloud for him.

The Bible became the primary source of my life. I realized very early that the Bible would be the difference between joy and happiness, defeat and victory, success and failure and peace and turmoil. As the head of my family I made sure that my children knew the importance of applying the Word of God to their lives.

During conversations with my sons, they frequently asked questions. My response usually began with: *"Son, what does the Bible say?"* One day my youngest son, Jeffrey, couldn't take it anymore, and said, *"Dad can't you ever answer a question without going to the Bible?"* My answer to him was a resounding, *"No"*.

It is critical that we know what the Bible says. The Bible is our guide for living. It is a practical book that gives general directions in every aspect of life. The best plan for your life is framed by the Word of God, the Bible.

The Bible states in Deuteronomy 6:6-9, *"And these words, which I command thee this day, shall be in thine heart: And thou shalt teach them diligently unto thy children, and shalt talk of them when thou sittest in thine house, and when thou walkest by the way, and when thou liest down, and when thou riseth up. And thou shalt bind them for a sign upon thine hand, and they shall be as frontlets between thine eyes. And thou shalt write them upon the posts of thy house, and on thy gates."*

The Holy Scripture is our primary source for living, whether you are young, old, rich or poor. From nation-to-nation, generation-to-generation, His Word remains the same.

PUSHED TO DESTINY

**Weeping may endure for a night,
but joy cometh in the morning.
Psalm 30:5b**

I love the saints and know they basically mean well. I remember the days when their 'good-intentions' almost cost us dearly. Unknowingly, the saints created extreme stress for my wife. It seemed their first order of business was to run my wife's life. I had young members, saved and unsaved. No one was taught church etiquette. Consequently we made many mistakes. Some of the saints took their mission so serious that they came to our home and instructed, *"You are the Pastor's wife. You ought to do this and you ought to do that."* Thank God for the intervention of the Holy Ghost.

When God saw that my wife could take no more, He told me to move. I responded, *"God, I have no where to go."* In obedience to God, I deposited $100.00 for a house located on Nathaniel Place. I had exactly $52.00 left, which the church gave me during the church's anniversary. The very next day, God sent a sister to us. She said that she and her husband were having a house built in North Chicago. They no longer wanted to move, but desired to give us the home.

My wife and I, accompanied by Brother and Sister Anderson, went to the site where the house was being built. When we walked on the planks of the house, the Brother prayed. When he finished praying, God confirmed His word and said, *"The house is yours."*

Mr. Chatman, the builder, told me to have my wife meet with the decorators to select the colors and tiles she desired. I told him that I did not have any money. He replied that he didn't ask me for money. On January 16, 1960, my family and I moved into a brand new house without paying one nickel. We rejoiced as we dwelled in the house the Lord provided.

After a month, I assumed someone would come for the rent, but no one did. After three months a man came and told me I needed a down payment. I asked him, *"How much?"* He said I would need $2,000. He asked me how much I had. I didn't have any money. However, I had a profit sharing account at Sears where I could withdraw only $1,100. I told the man that I could give him $1,100. He accepted that and said we could pay the $900 over a two-year period by adding it to the mortgage. Miraculously my mortgage was $126 a month, plus an additional $40 for two years.

Earlier in life I declared that I would own a house by the time I reached age 25. Here I was, one month after my 25th birthday, a blessed homeowner.

Yes, weeping may endure for a night, but joy does come. The sufferings are not worthy to be compared with the glory that is revealed in us. My wife and I have grown in the grace and the knowledge of our Lord and Saviour Jesus Christ. I have learned how to esteem my wife above myself. The saints have learned that God is the author and finisher of my wife's faith. We reaped the blessings of God as we walked in obedience to His commands.

The Lord requires us to trust Him with all of our heart and lean not unto our own understanding. In all our ways we must acknowledge Him and He will direct our paths. He didn't give those instructions just to hear Himself speak; He will test you. When the Lord told me to sell our house in North Chicago, Illinois, we had just finished redecorating. We had remodeled the kitchen and placed murals on one of the walls. Everything reflected our personality. We were content and felt 'at home'. But I said, *"Lord, if you give us a buyer, we will sell."*

Within two weeks, a man from Evanston, Illinois bought our house. We decided to move forward. I gave our earnest money to the realtor towards a house on Oak Street in Evanston. However, when we arrived in

Evanston, I learned that my check bounced and the deal fell through.

There I was with a wife and four children and no place to live. We had no other choice. We moved in with my mom, stepfather, and two sisters, in Maywood, Illinois. There were four adults and six kids in a two-bedroom home. We stayed for six months. Then we moved to a greasy, dirty, roach-infested townhouse located on Dempster Street in Evanston, Illinois.

The saints were wonderful. They helped us clean the place until it was livable. Finally, we settled into our townhouse apartment. Shortly afterwards, I had to minister in India. While I was away, the landlord sold the townhouse and gave us thirty days to move. I prayed and told the Lord, *"You've got to do something."* God sent us Mary, a lady that worked at the North Shore Hotel, and she said, *"We have a kitchenette apartment that you can move into."* We moved into it but after three months, we had to move from that place.

Finally, the only place I could find was the little house owned by the church. Randy Roebuck's mother and her children had lived there. Because my wife almost had a nervous breakdown the first time we lived close to the church, she said, *"I can't stay there."* We prayed that God would comfort Baby during this difficult time. The Lord answered our prayer. He caused the saints to be extremely nice. We stayed there for nine months, and during that time, they gave us our privacy.

Knowing that we could not reside in that little house

forever, we continued investigating avenues to purchase a home. We realized that 'Trusting God' for a roof over our heads had become a routine way of life for us; and when it didn't look like God was with us, we still had to 'Trust Him'.

We prayed about a house again, and the Lord sent me to a crook to have my house built. I recognized the voice of God and I obeyed. Who was I to question God? I knew the man I was going to was a crook. The community knew he was a crook. In fact, he knew he was a crook. So, he did what crooks do, stole my money. He dug the basement, poured the foundation and quit working. Then I decided, whether I lived, died, sunk, or swam, I was not giving this man another dime. Adding insult to injury, after only a year the foundation cracked in four places. Weeds began to grow through the cracks. Even with great faith I could not see this as our home.

Once again I started to look for a place to live. We thought we found a place so we proceeded with the paperwork. While in the realtor's office trying to buy the house, the Holy Spirit said, "No". I got up and said, "Never mind", and we walked out of the door. I guess the man thought that I was crazy and my wife may have thought so too. But all things work together for good for those who love the Lord and are called according to his purpose. Crazy or not, I stepped out on faith to follow the Lord's plan.

Shortly thereafter the Lord sent a man who agreed to complete the construction of our original house. In 1972, our house was finished and we moved into our new home.

MAN-TO-MAN

Mark the perfect man, and behold the upright:
for the end of that man is peace.
Psalm 37:37

My wife came from a strong Christian background. She received her spiritual nurturing at St. Luke Church of God in Christ in Chicago, Illinois.

I thank God for her very gentle spirit. I am the first to admit that I would not be the person I am in ministry if she had not helped me. She never tells me what to do, but she so sweetly makes suggestions, which are usually prefaced by, 'But Honey'.

At times when we were not even talking and during the most inopportune moment, my wife would begin a conversation with 'But Honey'. Her comments were as if there had been a conversation in progress. I could only conclude that a conversation was going on in her mind. Usually when she began a conversation with 'But Honey' she was concerned about something that was disturbing her, or there was a decision that needed to be made. 'But Honey' indicated the seriousness of what was on her mind. It meant that she wanted my undivided attention.

I could be in bed, sound asleep when I would hear her say, 'But Honey'; immediately, I would wake up because I knew she desired my attention. I knew that she wanted to talk. I have never ignored her need for me to listen to her. For more than thirty years I have traveled limitlessly, sometimes completing more than twelve trips in a month. It was important that I made myself available to Baby when I was home. Some issues she needed to discuss were on her mind since I left for the trip.

I encourage every spouse, male and female, to be sensitive to the non-verbal language spoken by their spouse.

The Holy Spirit taught me to be sensitive. Without a doubt, I love my wife, but early in our marriage I believed that my work as a preacher was more important. My belief was evident because my actions supported it. I left home early in the morning to do 'the Lord's work' and stayed until late at night, without calling her. I was spiritual enough to pray until drug addicts were delivered, but not sensitive enough to call my wife and tell her where I was. Some nights she paced the floor until 2:00 a.m., wondering if anything had happened to me. The Holy Spirit showed me how to sensitize myself to my wife. His work was not yet finished.

In the early days, my beliefs had to be refined and the Holy Spirit was right there to do it. I was a preacher and as such, I should arrive to church on time, regardless of what it took. When we prepared for church, I dressed myself while my wife dressed the four children and herself. They knew they must be ready to leave when I said so. It was extremely stressful trying to get five people dressed according to my time schedule. She knew I would leave them if they were not ready. One morning, after deciding to wait no longer, I left her with her shoe in one hand. As I went down the stairs, the Holy Spirit stopped me and said, *"Go back."* When I reentered the room, I saw my wife standing helpless with one shoe and stocking in her hands, as the tears rolled down her face. That morning the Holy Spirit knocked all the fire out of 'my importance'. I repented to God and her and then asked, *"Baby, what can I do to help you?"* God was teaching me. I realized I was a pastor with a wife and babies who had to balance the church and my family. The Holy Spirit made me so sensitive to the intricate needs and the smallest details of my wife and children that I started keeping safety pins in my pants in case Baby needed one for the children.

I live by the word of God. If the Bible says it is wrong, I don't have to be convinced. It is settled immediately. We must continually remind ourselves, and each generation about the sanctity of marriage. The Bible makes no allowance for couples to live together as husband and wife, while they are unmarried. Yesterday, we called it 'shacking', today it is 'cohabitating'. Simply stated, it is 'sin'.

In one of the tent meetings God ordained that I preach against living together. As I preached, my assistant pastor's wife walked out. After service, I was talking with the assistant pastor when I asked, *"Where is your wife?"* He informed me that she was not his wife, and he was in-love outside of his marriage. He further stated that he wanted to have babies and his wife couldn't so he got involved with this sister. Needless to say, I removed him from the assistant pastor position the next day.

Some of our church members experienced domestic violence. One sister's husband constantly beat her. One day, she rose up and fought back. She shot him in the foot. The police were called and she was arrested, but later released because it was ruled 'self-defense'.

I discovered that many sisters were abused by their husbands. They accepted it just to keep him. They refused to tell anyone that the brothers were slapping them around. When the abuse left visible scars, the wives told the saints all sorts of lies to cover up the abuse.

A wife who suffers abuse at the hands of her 'saved' husband should tell everyone, *"He's the one who bruised me."* Then the church will be able to help. The wife is not helping her abusive husband when she pretends all is well and returns home to another beating.

I do not preach longsuffering to a wife whose husband constantly beats her. I will not advise her to stay until the Lord brings her out. Proverbs 16:32 states, *"A man that ruleth his spirit is better than he that taketh a city."* Hence, you ought to be able to control your spirit to prevent the possibility of abusing anyone. There were cases where a sister ran her husband away. Every man did not leave his home because he wanted to; he just wanted to find peace.

I praise God that my wife and I never had a serious

argument. When I was really angry, I would keep silent, because spoken words can never be retracted and angry words leave deep scars. It has always been easy for me to repent to my wife, and ask for her forgiveness. This kept the atmosphere clear between us. Saying, *"I'm sorry"* does not cost anything. Some men would rather go out and buy a yacht and put it on dry land rather than say, *"I'm sorry"*. Some men find it painful to humble themselves and admit that they are wrong, but when they do, they must admit that the results were worth the pain.

If my wife and I had separated during our time of struggle, Faith Temple would not exist neither would the years of love that we have shared. Our problems were as real as any other couple's. However, we loved each other and knew that with love, we could make it. We applied the word of God to every situation. When we finished looking at our problems in light of God's word, we realized that we were human, filled with flaws. It did not matter who was right or wrong. Casting blame profits nothing. What mattered was that we both were sorry and wanted to move beyond our challenges.

My wife is a very talented lady. As a professional seamstress, Baby sewed many different types of clothing. A sister at the church, Mary Armstead, told us about a thrift shop in Highland Park, Illinois where rich women consigned their clothes. The thrift shop was a blessing. My wife could get a $10.00 dress and tailor it to look like a $200.00 dress. I only earned $44.00 a week, so going to expensive stores to shop was out of the question. Her thrifty shopping enabled me to be the sole provider for our family.

I was determined that my wife would not work. Every week I gave her money for herself. I never asked her how much money she had. I did not marry for her to take care of me. My vow was to care for her. I wanted to be a godly man and husband.

I admonish the brothers to give their wives money, whether she works or not. If they do not give her any money, then they are not providing for her. They must understand that providing is more than food, shelter and clothing. It must also be understood that women love to be appreciated and valued. Their value should primarily be in who she is and not what she does. Above all, every man should know that a woman's worth is not in sex because most women can live without it.

After awhile, your wife will think that if she has to buy her own clothes and food or pay for her own car, she might as well be alone. It does not matter how much a brother earns, he needs to give his wife money, even if he has to borrow it or go without. This unselfish act tells your wife, *"I care about you."* I do not tell Baby how to spend the money that I give her, I just want her to know that I care.

Marriage is honorable and it is an Art; however, it is a job also. Marriage requires work and more work. We must work to make marriage work. We must communicate to understand the requirements and roles within our marriages. Communication prevents misunderstandings; nevertheless, a large percentage of domestic problems are a result of misunderstandings between husbands and wives.

To illustrate, there was such a case in the church with a sister who loved God and desired to obey the Bible. One day, without her husband's knowledge, she went to the bank and withdrew $2,800. She had the cashier's check written in the name of the church, but she gave it to a visiting preacher. But the preacher could not cash it because it was written to the church.

Later that evening her husband came to my house. He was crying and very angry. Despite his anger, I saw the pain of his disappointment. He asked me where he could find the preacher because he wanted to kill him. I tried to explain that it was not the preacher's fault, but he refused to listen. Finally, I told him that the check was at the church and if he would come to the church, I would give it to him. He then calmed down and agreed to the arrangement.

I recognized that we had a serious situation. We had a wife who had given away their life's savings. She made a very serious decision without discussing it with her husband. And we had a husband filled with anger and murder in his heart. The next morning, the visiting preacher came to the church for his check, only to find out that we were giving it back. He was very disappointed.

I asked the husband not to remain angry with his

wife. She expressed that she had not done anything for the church. Since they had the money, she wanted to give it to the church. As a result, he decided that his wife could no longer come to the church. I advised her to obey her husband. Since she could not come to church, we took communion to her every Monday following communion service. This continued for an entire year. Then one Sunday morning, to her surprise, her husband woke up and said, "Aren't you going to church?" She returned to church rejoicing because God had delivered her.

New situations developed constantly. My wife and I had to get one woman from her boyfriend's house before her husband realized what was happening. During the war, her husband was out at sea and she began seeing another man. This man came along when she was very vulnerable. He convinced her to move in with him. We knew that she loved her husband and that her husband loved her. Baby and I went to the Great Lakes Navel Base, where she and her lover were living. We packed her bags and took her home. There she awaited her husband's return. I have learned that some people will come out of bad situations if they have someone to help them.

We also had a young man who just couldn't cope with the issues of life. Anytime he was unable to get along with his wife, he would slash his wrist. This became a regular occurrence until one night about 3:00a.m., he called me. I drove to his home, picked him up, and brought him to our house. My wife administered first aid. Afterwards, I talked with him until he gave his life to the Lord. When we finished praying, he said, "I don't feel like killing myself anymore. I feel like living."

TESTIMONIES

I JUST WANT TO TESTIFY

To testify means to put God on display. To show how powerful and mighty He is. We testify of things that we have personally seen or experienced. Our lives testify of the reality of God in the earth. This section contains a few testimonies of what God has done in my life. I pray that you are encouraged to trust God even more than you did yesterday.

God's Healing Compassion

Beloved, I wish above all things that thou
mayest prosper and be in health...
III John 2

As a young boy, I suffered with epileptic seizures. Thus, someone had to accompany me everywhere I went. While walking down the street, the enemy would suddenly inflict my body with a seizure. I would find myself lying in the street. But one day, Jesus Christ of Nazareth, the Son of God, healed me. I don't know when or where, but one thing I do know is that I am healed.

I also suffered with sinus trouble so badly that I was forced to lay flat on my back for two weeks. One day I told my mother that if she took me to the church, the Lord would heal me. She called for Uncle John who came and wrapped me in a pink and white blanket and took me to church. He sat me in the middle of the service. No one laid their hand on me and prayed. When Elder Markham asked me to speak, I got up and stood by the altar. As I spoke, God touched me. He removed the root cause of the ailment. To God be the glory!

One day, Baby became very ill. The doctors explained that she needed an operation and there were certain steps that must be carried out before the operation. The doctors did not realize that the steps of a good man are ordered by the Lord. Before the doctors had a chance to do what they thought was necessary, God intervened. One night while taking Holy Communion, God instantly healed her. This is why the Lord's Supper is so important and special to me. It serves as a memorial of Jesus' death and my wife's healing.

In 1971, shortly after my return from a mission trip to India, I began suffering from back pain. I will not say that it was a demonic attack, but I will not rule it out either. While in India, I went with a native, Brother Joi, to visit the Hindu Temple. We were looking at some of the gods they worshipped, which included a large tree with blood stains. As we stood there, discussing the stronghold the devil had on the people, I stepped back slightly to get a full view of the tree. In doing so, I fell backwards into the courtyard. That began years of suffering with back pain.

When I returned home, I dealt with the pain as well as possible. Each day the pain seemed to increase, but I never stopped fulfilling the call God placed on my life. In 1972, I traveled to Sweden for a 14-day revival. The pain in my back intensified. Now I was suffering from a pinched sciatic nerve, blood in my stool, back hurting terribly, and pain in my legs. The doctor later confirmed the pinched sciatic nerve and blood in my stool.

To deal with the pain, I laid on the floor, propped my feet up, and prayed. I was in excruciating pain, but I still had nine days left to preach. I preached every day, two times a day. When I lost my equilibrium, I leaned on anything that was available and continued to preach until I was finished. When I returned home, my wife took me to the hospital. I was placed in traction for a week. Everything went well and I was able to return to ministering.

In January 1973, my back went out again. It was never really healed; the doctors could only provide temporary relief. The back pain progressed from bad to worse. I would experience muscle spasms where I could not bend my back at all. That's when Pastor Don Lyons introduced me to a chiropractic clinic in Rockford, Illinois. While attending the clinic, he allowed me to stay in one of his guest houses. I was there for three weeks. Elder Randolph Moore was responsible for overseeing the church while I was gone. I came home feeling much better. I thought all was well. My mother even had a dream that the Lord healed me.

Shortly after being released from the clinic, I was invited to preach in Maywood, Illinois. My daughter drove me to the church. I preached and felt wonderful. I returned home and went to bed. At approximately 3:00a.m., I woke up in such pain that I thought I would die. My wife rushed me to Victory Memorial Hospital in Waukegan, Illinois.

My doctor, Dr. S. P. Kaiz, was called. He was my family doctor before I was married. X-rays showed that I suffered from a deteriorating disc. Something was resting on the nerve and to correct it would require surgery. My doctor informed me that if I did not consent to the surgery, I would have to live with the pain for the rest of my life.

After being in the hospital, in traction, for fourteen days, I asked my doctor if it were him would he have the operation. He honestly said he would have to give it a lot of thought. I told him that I had already given it a lot of thought and was not going to have the operation. After two weeks of hospital confinement, I decided that if the Lord did not heal me, I would not be healed.

Wednesday morning I got up, released myself from the traction, and took a shower. On the way back to bed, while holding on to the rod along the wall of my room, I felt warmth travel up my back. At that moment I knew the Lord was touching my back. Suddenly, I realized that all of the pain and discomfort in my back had vanished. I was instantly healed and made whole. My doctor came into my room and asked me what I planned to do. I told him that I was going home. He said, *"Okay, but let me run some more tests first."* When his tests and analysis were completed, he returned and said, *"I don't know what happened, but you can go home."* I never again experienced back pain or discomfort. Despite more than thirty years of extensive travel, lugging heavy suitcases and sitting for long hours on flights, I never again endured any form of back pain. God healed me with His compassion.

The Secret and the Miracle

...My God shall supply all your need...
Philippians 4:19

I know what it is to be poor, but I didn't have a poverty mentality. My father never did anything for me but I still had integrity. Sometimes I had to place a piece of cardboard on the inside of my shoes because the soles had holes in them. But I would shine them and go on my way, with my head held high. One day while kneeling at the altar praying, I forgot to position my feet so that the holes in my shoes could not be seen. One of the Brothers at church, named Robert Gill, Sr., saw the holes, but he never said a word. He immediately went downtown and bought me a pair of shoes. The ones he purchased were made with very thick soles. I guess he wanted to make sure it would be a long time before I had holes in my shoes again.

Many years later, what could be seen on the sole of my shoe wasn't a hole, but a miracle! I had gone on a mission trip to Athens, Greece. The mission team and I climbed Mars Hill to look over the city. While on Mars Hill, I became so excited because I was on the very hill that the Apostle Paul preached on. When we returned to the hotel and I removed my shoes, the Holy Spirit had me to look under my shoe. I was amazed at what I saw! I showed my son, Carlis Jr., and he too looked at the shoe in amazement. Then I rubbed the bottom of the shoe.

It felt completely smooth as if they were practically new shoes. After rubbing the shoe, what I saw was still there! There was an imprint of a cross under my shoe!

The next morning I woke up and the cross was still there. I wore the shoes when I was going to meet the rest of the mission team. When we met, I removed my shoes and showed them the miracle that had taken place! Many of them looked and photographed this special miracle. After two days, the cross was gone. To think, I was excited about being where the Apostle Paul preached, but God was showing me that His Presence was there with me.

THE WEARY TRAVELER

...some have entertained angels unawares.
Hebrews 13:2

One morning, my family had just sat down to breakfast when the doorbell rang. I answered the door and there was a hobo who had come to the house looking for something to eat. He was tattered and smelly. As he stood in the doorway cold and hungry, I had to make a decision. Would I disregard the safety of my wife and babies to warm and feed a stranger? I thought, *"He could be a thief or anything."* But my heart said, *"He came all the way from the train tracks to my house. He passed many other houses on the way, and did not stop until he reached mine."*

Then I considered God's Word, which states, *"Some have entertained angels unaware."* So I said to the stranger, *"Come in and have a seat."* He sat down and had breakfast with us. Afterwards, my wife prepared a little lunch for him to take on his journey. We blessed him and he left. It is true that the Lord watched over us; but it is also true that He used us to meet the needs of that stranger. Was the stranger a hobo or an angel, only God knows!

THE WHISPERER

...a whisperer separateth chief friends.
Proverbs 16:28

I learned early that with spiritual growth comes demonic attacks. By nature, I am not easily upset. However, there was an incident, early in my ministry, which made me angry, almost instantly.

One Sunday morning a young lady came to Evanston to see me. We were in Sunday school so she patiently waited. Afterwards, she whispered to me that she wanted to pray for me. I did not have a problem with people laying hands on me because I believed what was within me was greater than any outside force. I waited and watched as the young lady placed a chair in the middle of the floor and asked me to sit. She anointed me and began to pray. After she prayed, she whispered in my ear, *"The Lord said, 'Leave her alone'."* In fury, I jumped up and demanded, *"Leave who alone?"* She tried to quiet me down saying, *"sssh, sssh, sssh."* She began to speak again saying, *"The Lord said......"* I interrupted her and said, *"You go back and tell your lord I said, "He lied."* At that point she became real nervous, gathered her things and ran out of the church. From the day I dedicated my life to Jesus I had lived clean before Him and no devil in hell was going to tarnish my name or God's glory.

STAND

Stand fast therefore in the liberty wherewith Christ hath made us free, and be not entangled again with the yoke of bondage.
Galatians 5:1

When I was in school, I refused to participate in physical education, sporting events, or wear the attire for such activities. My refusal was based on my spiritual convictions. I did not ask my mother, I took a stand. My firmness helped establish needed changes for Christians in public school.

A generation later, when my son, Carlis, was in school, I attended a meeting with his counselor to protest his reading of a book entitled, 'Catcher in the Rye'. The book contained excessive profanity and I determined that it was too unclean for my son. The counselor gave me two options. Either he reads the book and prepares a report, or he fails the class. During the discussion with the counselor, I simply used the wisdom of God to overpower earthly wisdom. I asked one question: *"If I allow my son to read this book, and he comes to school one day and uses some of the profane words from this book to the teacher, what will happen to him?"* She answered, *"He'll be punished."* I agreed and said, *"That is exactly why I will not permit my son to read the book."* I then requested that my son be provided a decent book to read and report on; AND IT WAS SO!

There is a true adage, *"If you don't stand for something, you'll fall for everything."* The things that are seen are temporal, but the things that are not seen are eternal. The power of God that worked in me helped change that situation.

THE TRANSITORY WORLD

...there is no new thing under the sun.
Ecclesiastes 1:9b

It would have been easy for me to be bitter towards Caucasians. While working at a well-known department store, I was given a daily dose of prejudice. Day after day, I dealt with the racial slurs and remarks. Of course, they assured me that their comments pertained to other blacks, not me. I was one of the good 'ole' boys. I was somehow different than the rest of the black race. Yes, and if I believed that, I'm sure that they would have sold me another bill of goods.

One day, like many others, racism raised its ugly head and I could take it no longer. I confronted my accuser. God gave me the words to say: *"If you hate us so much, why do you spend so much money and time in the sun trying to look like us?"* When I spoke those words, the man was speechless. God's wisdom helped reduce future racist remarks.

During my adolescence, I attended segregated schools until I moved to Waukegan, Illinois. In the Waukegan school, kids willingly shared everything. Regardless of their skin color and gender, each child learned from the same book as I. We studied our lessons step by step, each at our own pace. Although this was very new for me, I was encouraged. God then spoke to my heart and told me that He would do for us, as Blacks, what He had done for our forefathers. He would send deliverance.

Ironically, we believed that when we were finally integrated, everything would be all right. Thousands lost their lives for racial equality. We wanted integration. The many fatalities brought us integrated schools, dormitories, cities and towns. Now, a new thought is on the horizon. Today, we want to revert back to segregation. This is a transitory world. Before, we wanted unification, the same things and the same quality of life. Now, we want separation. Real stability will only take place through a commitment to Jesus Christ as Saviour

SNATCHED FROM HELL

...the violent take it by force.
Matthew 11:12

Many things happen and the preacher is sometimes the last to know. My prayer is that the saints would realize that the preacher watches for their soul and has only their eternal best interest at heart. I remember when Baby and I learned that one of our brothers was practicing occultism. We went to Main Street where he lived. We were going to get him. We heard that he and a girl moved in together and sat up an altar to Buddha. When we arrived, I said to him, *"You and I do not believe that Buddha is God. Come out of here."* Baby and I packed his bags and took him away. He never returned to the occult.

COUNT YOUR BLESSINGS

...and pour you out a blessing, that there
shall not be room enough to receive it.
Malachi 3:10b

On June 7, 2002 at 3:07 p.m., I was sitting in my office talking on the telephone. It was as if an electric shock hit me. At first I thought that it was from my computer malfunctioning. The shock traveled from the top of my head down to my face and then to my hand. During this entire time, I continued to talk on the telephone. I began to look around because I sensed that something was wrong. As the shock reached my hand, it went limp and I dropped the telephone. I picked it up again and continued to talk. When the shock reached my hand again, it went limp and I dropped the telephone a second time. By this time, I was sure that I was having a stroke. At that moment, I lifted my hand and shouted, "Loose Me"!

The shout was so strong and loud that my secretary, Sister Barbara Woodards, came running to see what was wrong. My son, Anthony Charles, came into my office and immediately called the paramedics. When they arrived, I walked to the stretcher and they strapped me down. My face was twisted and my right eye was closed.

At the hospital, Pastor John Brewer and Elder George Woodards prayed for me and immediately there was noticeable improvement in my face and eye. During the time I spent in the emergency room, I had little concern and gave no real thought to the fact that I had endured a deadly stroke. I was more concerned about whether or not I would be able to continue preaching with a distorted face.

After completing some x-rays, the doctors discovered a hole in my heart. They determined that it had been there, undetected, since I was a child. With all of the x-rays that I have had in my lifetime, I knew that God had a purpose for this discovery on this day, at this time. The doctors explained that a blood clot traveled through the hole in my heart to my brain and caused the stroke. They also stated that if it had not been for the hole in my heart, I would have had a massive heart attack and died!

I entered the hospital on a Thursday and came home on the following Wednesday. The Lord God is indeed my Healer!

Now that the hole in my heart had been detected, my caregiver, Carmen Watson, a nurse from my church, strongly recommended that I receive the operation, which would repair the hole in my heart. On September 27, 2002, I decided to have the doctors investigate the impact of repairing the hole in my heart. They determined that the process should have minimal complications since the passage to the heart had no blockage. On September 28, 2002, I went through all of the preparation for my upcoming surgery. On Friday, I was put to sleep, opened up and the hole in my heart repaired. It was a 9-inch laceration and a four-hour operation. While in recovery, I began to experience internal hemorrhaging. The doctors had to re-open the laceration and address the hemorrhage. I slept through the entire ordeal. When I awoke, I knew nothing about what had happened. When the doctors tried to prescribe medication to lessen the pain from the surgery, I told them that I did not feel any pain. They were speechless! From that day until now, I have not felt any pain or taken a single pain pill. Our God is the Great Physician!

During the 2004 Pastor's Appreciation Breakfast, it was announced that I was unanimously selected to receive the biennial award of an Honorary Doctorate of Divinity. I was shocked! Never could I have imagined receiving such a distinguished honor. This prestigious accolade is given by the Interdenominational Theological Center/Charles Mason Theological Seminary. The official award ceremony was held on May 7, 2005 in Atlanta, Georgia.

Only God knows how to orchestrate 'The Perfect' Celebration. On Saturday, September 3, 1955, Baby and I were married and on Saturday, September 3, 2005, exactly fifty years later, we reaffirmed our wedding vows. The late Elder Luke Austin performed our original wedding ceremony. His son, Bishop James Curtis Austin, performed our reaffirmation ceremony. Our wedding theme was 'Through the Years'. I have thanked God over and over for such an awesome day of celebration and remembrance. One of our church mothers, Mother June Huff, wrote us the most befitting poem:

A Marriage Made in Heaven

**"Rise up my love, My fair one,
and come away".
Song of Solomon 2:10**

She heard the voice of her Beloved,

Fifty long years ago –

When He bade her to "rise up".

She would not tell him "no".

Using the sweet title of "My Love",

Meant that he counted her fair,

And so, his call to "come away",

Had no harsh sound in her ear.

Their marriage took place in September,

Hand in hand to walk this way –

Their faithfulness and dedication,

Are what brings us here today.

Copyright 2005
June Huff

THE PASTOR

Pastoring is what I do and who I am!
A Good Shepherd cares for his sheep!

THE STRAIGHT PATH
WHICH SEEMED CROOKED

And we know that all things work
together for good...
Romans 8:28

Originally, I came to Evanston to sing and support a church's music ministry. I never intended to settle there. I had planned to become an evangelist and travel around the world preaching the gospel of Jesus Christ.

As believers, I recognize that we are to always pray. Hence, when I enter a church or a saint's home, I routinely kneel and pray. One Sunday afternoon I attended a service at Second Baptist church. As was my custom, I knelt and prayed. That night I met Mother Sadie Adams and her daughter, Thelma Adams, who greatly influenced my life. Mother Adams was a Mother at the St. Paul Church of God in Christ in Chicago, Illinois. Thelma was the choir director at Springfield Missionary Baptist church in Evanston, Illinois. At the conclusion of the service, Thelma came to me and asked, *"Are you Church of God in Christ?"* I answered, *"Yes"*. She responded, *"I am in the Church of God in Christ too"*. Our common background inspired her to ask the church's pastor to invite me to preach. He did, and that invitation led to many others.

While periodically preaching there for a number of years, I became a frequent dinner guest in the home of Mother Adams. One day she said to me, *"There are a lot of backsliders in Evanston. They were saved and loved the Lord, but they are no longer walking with Him. We need a church here. I hope that the Lord will send you here to start a church"*. Start a church? That was the furthest thing from my mind. I wanted to be an evangelist so I dismissed her remarks. But whether I liked it or not, God had birthed in my spirit the desire to pastor, the night I met Mother Adams when I knelt to pray.

At age thirteen, my mom, my stepfather, Elder Adams and I lived in Chicago. Elder Jessie Campbell gave me my first opportunity to preach during a revival. After that revival, the Campbell family became my family. They received me with open arms and treated me like a birth member of their family.

Later Bishop W.D.C. Williams of Evanston, Illinois invited me to his church. After I had visited for a while, his oldest daughter taught me how to play the organ. From 1952 through 1957, I preached as a guest minister in all of the African American churches in Evanston; specifically, Bethel, Mt. Carmel, Tabernacle Baptist, Ebenezer, Second Baptist, Springfield, Faith Tabernacle, and Mt. Zion.

I also preached in the streets: at the corner of Church and Dodge, in front of Evanston Township High School, and on the corner near the Foster Community Center.

In January 1957, six months after the birth of our first child, I was appointed pastor of the Faith Temple Church of God in Christ at Evanston. Bishop Louis Henry Ford appointed me to the position. I was twenty-two years old. The church began with six members. When I left Greater St. James Church of God in Christ, I only took my wife and our daughter. My mother joined us later. Since I was a faithful servant under Elder Markham's leadership, when God sent me forth He blessed my ministry. Today, there are approximately five hundred members.

Three days after starting the new church, my faith was tested. My wife and I, along with our daughter, lived with my mother and her brother Richard. Finances were tight. My mother and I had debts, which I could not repay. Although I longed for a private family life with Baby, Sideary and I, I felt obligated to stay with my mother until the debts were paid in full.

At approximately 5:30 a.m., my wife woke me and said, *"Honey, the house is on fire"*. I responded, *"Baby, the house is not on fire, it's probably Uncle John burning something in the furnace"*. But she said again, *"Honey, I think the house is on fire"*. At that point I decided to investigate and sure enough, the house was on fire. I grabbed my pants and top coat and took my family to safety. We stood and watched our home go up in flames. Unfortunately, there was no insurance on the house or on our furniture; all was gone.

I was employed by Sears and Roebuck at that time. When my employer heard of our loss, he granted me permission to go through the store and pick out whatever clothing my family and I needed. The church, God's people, also came to our aide. Their gifts included money, which was truly pressed down, shaken together and running over, for it paid all of our debts. Baby, Sideary and I were also delivered from an uncomfortable living arrangement. When He who had begun a good work was finished, our latter house was greater than our former house!

At the time I was establishing Faith Temple Church of God in Christ at Evanston, Illinois, I was young and filled with zeal. Most of the members were also young. God then sent Deacon Tate, Mother Maggie Logan, and Sister Drennen to us. These saints were older, wiser, and stable. Mother Gatin, who was not a member, would routinely come and pray for the church. She often said, *"I'm so glad ain't nobody God but God"*. I was so blessed to have those types of saints. They were saints who studied the Word and loved to pray. Since Mother Logan ate, slept, and lived the Word, I sent many people to her home for counseling. From the beginning of our ministry, God sent saints like Mother Lillie Hudson, Mother Jones, and our church mother, Mother Sadie Adams. These mothers treated Baby and I like their son and daughter.

God sent them to help me slow down and live longer. I had established a pace where I would convert the whole city in one day. Deacon Tate, Mother Logan, and Sister Drennen had lived in Evanston for many years and knew that I would not accomplish that goal. They simply prayed for me. I would hear them sometimes praying to the Lord asking Him to give me strength, wisdom, and a settled spirit. Finally, I realized that the city of Evanston would not be saved in a single day. Nevertheless, I knew that my job was to preach.

God allowed me to attain wisdom as I sat with the Elders. I valued the wisdom of the old and I understood that true wisdom coincided with God's Word. Although I was a saved young man, I was old in character. I was always serious. I did not practice joking. If something did not align with the Word it was foolishness and I had no part of it because the old saints said that jesting was a sin. And I did not want sin in my life.

My job was to preach, not entertain. I took my responsibility very seriously and preached with all my heart. After four years of ministry we had a membership of only fifteen. However, I had two things on my side: nerve and the Holy Spirit.

My wife and I shared an intense love for the ministry and God's people. The care of the church weighed heavily upon our hearts. We believed that we were fulfilling the will of God, though we witnessed very little increase in our ministry. We lived in North Chicago, the church was in Evanston, and it had not grown the way we expected. We needed a fresh word from the Lord. We desired to hear from Heaven. We prayed, told God about our situation, and asked Him for direction.

While waiting to hear from Him, we continued driving thirty miles from North Chicago to church in Evanston. Often times only two people would be there, Sister Johnnie Hicks and Sister Cammie Ross. I would preach just as hard to them as I would to a big crowd.

The number of people did not sway me one way or the other. Sometimes, my only audience was my wife and baby. My convictions kept me strong. I knew that my preaching was not in vain because God told me to preach.

On my secular job, I worked an average of eight to twelve hours a day. After leaving work I went home, changed clothes, and went to church. We arrived only to find an average of two people in attendance. Nevertheless, we remained faithful. I only missed church once in seven years and that was beyond my control. We were experiencing a huge snowstorm and the Lord told me to turn around and go home. When I arrived home and turned on the television, I discovered that a blizzard was on its way. It lasted for several days. We were thankful for the Lord's protection. Deep in our hearts we still yearned for a Word. One morning after prayer, my wife came to me and said, *"The Lord said, if you quit your secular job and work fulltime in the ministry, He will increase the members and bless the church."*

How could the Lord tell me to leave my secular job, the miracle job, which He had provided? Besides, the church consisted of fifteen members! As a working man, with a wife and four children, I was surviving. I couldn't imagine what a non-working man with a wife and four children would do. We had been in our home for seven years. *"How could we pay for a house, car, and build a church with just fifteen members?"* I asked myself. Despite the questions, I knew that the Lord said, *"Leave the job."* My wife's word from the Lord was confirmation. I obeyed the voice of the Lord and God has never failed to take care of us.

When I told my boss that I was quitting my job and devoting myself fulltime to the ministry, he told me that I was crazy. He asked, *"How many people do you have?"* I told him, *"About 16 or 17."* He then said, *"You are a fool. Those people can't support you."* I answered, *"Well, the Lord didn't say that they had to. He told me to leave my job and that's what I'm going to do."* In wisdom, I made the arrangements. I took my profit sharing and paid all of my bills with the exception of our home mortgage.

One day, shortly after leaving the job, the Lord visited me. I was setting up the tent in preparation for a revival. The Lord spoke to me and said, *"I will fill every chair you place under this tent."* I asked Brother Bonaparte, one of my trustees, to go and get more chairs. I told him what the Lord had said and asked him how many chairs he thought we should get. He said that we should fill it up. On Saturday afternoon he got 300 chairs. On Sunday night, every chair was filled! I preached deliverance and healing, reminding the people that Jesus Christ was the same yesterday, today, and forever.

During the revival, Sister Johnnie Hicks brought her sister, Sister Adrene Collins, and the rest of her family. For over twenty years, Sister Collins suffered with migraine headaches, leaving her with darkened eyes and black spots on her body. The blackening of her skin would occur wherever she felt pain. The doctor's prognosis was not good. Sister Collins took pills to decrease the pain and pills to sleep through the pain. That night, during the service, we prayed and the Lord healed her instantly. The next night she brought her medications to the church and placed them on the altar. From that moment, she never required medication for that illness again.

Because of this miraculous phenomenon, the people came from far and near. I preached and prayed for people every night for seven weeks. As God promised, He showed Himself strong in signs and wonders. One man was totally blind and the Lord gave him sight. A lady was blind in her left eye for nine years and God completely restored her vision.

I must confess that when they brought the blind man to me, my knees began to knock. There was no way for me to get out of praying for him, even though I tried. I repeatedly sent him to the back of the prayer line. After a few minutes, he was back up front again. So I asked him, *"What do you want from God?"* He said, *"I want to receive my sight."* I asked him, *"Do you believe that God will do it?"* He said, *"Yeah, that's why I came."* Then the enemy began speaking to my mind. He said, *"What are you going to do, if he doesn't see?"* I said, *"I'm going to pray and pray until he does."* The enemy said, *"What if you pray and pray and he still doesn't see?"* I responded, *"I'm going to pray some more."* So I prayed one time, took my handkerchief out to wave in front of him and said, *"What do you see?"* He said, *"I see you waving something in front of me."* I prayed again. As I laid hands on him, I felt the power of

God. Again I asked the man what he saw. This time he said, *"I see your hand and you have five fingers."*

We prayed for everyone and every condition. The lame walked and the deaf ears were opened. Fifty-three people accepted Christ as their personal Saviour. After preaching for seven weeks, I asked the saints whether we should continue; they said, *"Yes"* but the Lord said, *"Stop"*. I continued anyway and the next week a terrible storm arose, which ripped the tent in half. We had an awful time! When God says, *"Stop"*, He means stop.

When Faith Temple Church of God in Christ at Evanston first started, we had no place to meet for services. We started holding Tuesday night services in Mother Adams' living room, while Thursday night ministry was held in the Foster School. Our first official worship service was April 24, 1957, held in the Foster School's Little Theater. Our first offering was $124.00.

When we were unable to use the Foster School, Sister Marion Hudson or Mother Clemmie Walker opened their home. Mother Walker's husband was a gambler. He gambled on horse races. Mr. Walker was a very kind man despite the fact that he had not received Christ as his Saviour. Mr. Walker loved music, but he could not play an instrument. However, he owned a piano, which he had tuned so that I could play it during our services. I grew as fond of him as he had of me.

When Mr. Walker was dying, I accompanied Mother Walker to the hospital. People in the community knew that Mr. Walker, the gambler, kept large sums of money hidden in a box inside his house. It was also common knowledge that he was in the hospital at the point of death. While Mother Walker and I were at the hospital, someone broke into their house and stole all of Mr. Walker's money and possessions from the box. Mother Walker said that she did not know the value of what was in the box, so she purposed in her heart that she would simply keep praising the Lord.

We continued holding our services in multiple places until we received a permanent room at the Foster School. Since the permanent room was only for Sunday morning, we continued holding services at Mother Adams' house. There were people who told me that I would never build a church in Evanston. At times it seemed true, given the myriad of challenges we faced trying to secure a location. In addition, I sometimes had only my wife, Sister Mertrude Roebuck and her children, Randy, Gertrude, Albert, and Mary in service. Due to health problems, Mother Adams seldom came to church even though she was one of the trailblazers who helped start it. I constantly reminded myself that all these things did not matter because God sent me there.

What do you do when those around you are constantly asking, *"Are you sure God sent you here?"* There were some who wanted me in Evanston, others who did not, and those who did not care one way or the other. The enemy strategically tried to destroy the vision, but I realized that the Lord was ordering my footsteps.

A certain little lady came to me every Sunday and

reported all the things that were said about me and the church. Unfortunately, the comments were from members of a well-established Evanston Church. They spoke freely and negatively about Faith Temple in her presence. They thought her mental imbalance prevented her understanding; to the contrary. She would come to me and repeat all that was said. I did not allow the words to divert my attention or shake my trust. This was merely a weapon that the enemy tried to use to discourage me.

I remember the days when I had no one to talk to. My calling compelled me to preach every Sunday, whether I felt good or bad. I had to minister without allowing the bad times to show. Most people do not realize that the same things that hurt others hurt me too. I was very thankful to have Thelma to talk with and saints who prayed for me daily.

Thelma was Faith Temple's first Financial Secretary and Choir Directress. She was the daughter of Brother Adams and wife of Brother Tony Grandison. Brother Tony was a lover of Sunday school. Every Sunday morning he picked up kids for Sunday school. If they were not ready, he helped them get ready. He routinely carried shoe polish with him, one bottle of brown and a bottle of white. If the children's shoes were untidy, he polished them while their mothers finished dressing them. His motivation was to inspire the children to love Sunday school, as he did.

Thelma's brother, Gene Adams, was a bus driver and sometimes played the organ for the church. Some of the saints did not want him to play because they said he smoked cigarettes. What they did not realize was that Gene wore his bus uniform, which was smoky from the passengers. So often we wrongly judge people not realizing the lasting effects an incorrect judgment can have.

I continued with the work of the ministry that God charged to me. Since winning souls to Christ was my primary goal, I decided to do something different. When I was superintendent, of the Sunday school department, the district purchased a tent. I decided to use the tent to hold outdoor services. The tent went up in the summer of 1957.

I set up the tent at the corner of Dodge Avenue and Emerson Street. That became my pulpit to preach the Gospel and win the lost. During each service, I stood under the tent yelling and screaming, but there was no one there to listen. In retrospect, I was pitiful. Then one night, God in His mercy allowed Bishop Louis Ford to visit the tent. He brought a busload of people from Chicago to hear me.

I preached when no one was present and I preached when someone came. I preached until I got sick. I preached until my tonsils popped. I preached when I had the Asiatic flu. I preached when I was feeling well. I preached when people drove by and laughed at me. I also played the piano. Sometimes people would park their cars and sit and listen to the music. I became known as the song preacher.

With the tent ministry came many challenges. During the service, the police came. Two of them were Fuzzy, a rookie officer, and Babe Cooper, a veteran. Babe lived directly across from the tent. Every night a barrage of policemen came by because someone in the neighborhood called to complain about us 'disturbing the peace'. I did not stop preaching. I preached until the policemen left. I did not know them all by name, but I said, *"If you don't get saved, you will die and go to hell too."* They were kind because they stood in the back, waited until I finished preaching, and asked, *"Can we talk?"* They said, *"Reverend, you've got to close down a little earlier. The neighbors are saying that you are making too much noise".* The next night I would openly rebuke the neighbors for calling the police. This happened regularly, summer after summer. Each year the tent meeting began the last week of June and ended the last week in August. All summer the police came and asked me to be a little quieter because the citizens in the community complained. They often said, *"Reverend, we don't want to come, but we have to come. We are Officers of the City and the people are calling us, so we must come".* I told them, *"It's your responsibility to come; but it's my responsibility to preach".* I watched as God established His work. It wasn't easy, but I learned that if you stand up for what's right, God will stand up for you.

Towards the end of the summer, I was afflicted with the Asiatic flu. It confined me to the bed for ten days. I couldn't even take the tent down, and there was only one other male in the entire church. Brother Adams was the first deacon but he was an elderly man, so I did not expect him to take down the tent. A man from North Chicago agreed to go to Evanston and disassemble the tent. God always has a ram in the bush. Sadly, Brother Adams died the following year.

In the summer of 1958, we purchased an even larger tent and placed it on the Canal bank near the bridge. The old tent was 25x60 feet, but this tent was 40x100 feet. Elder Lawrence Parks from the People's Church of God in Christ in Chicago joined me, and we shared the preaching. He was a Pastor and an Evangelist, so he ran the revival for me. This was my second revival.

During this revival I received threats. Some citizens threatened to beat me up and even kill me. Others called the police almost every night. But I withstood the threats and preached anyway. When I needed strength, I said, *"Lord, I need your strength to preach"*. God was always faithful to provide His strength. I only weighed 130 pounds. Some called me 'Six O'clock' while Elder Fred Daniel called me 'Bones'. After God's refreshing, I didn't care about the threats, how small I was, or about dying. If I died, it would be for the sake of the Gospel. I believed that 'death for the Gospel' would be for my gain and I knew nothing about the word 'martyr'. The issue was settled in my heart, but no one ever carried out the threats.

Using the Tent worked great for the summer, but we needed a place where we could hold our church services during the other months. I decided to ask some of the neighborhood churches to use their facility when they were not. Despite my diligent search, all of the male pastors turned me down. God allowed a lady pastor to open her church doors to us. We were permitted to use Faith Tabernacle Fire Baptize Holiness Church where Mother McCrackin was the Pastor. As we see in the Bible, God always has and will continue to use women. It would be hypocritical for me to speak against ladies in the ministry since God used a lady to bless me when I needed it most.

ONLY TWO OPTIONS

As the mountains are round about
Jerusalem, so the Lord is round about
His people from henceforth even forever.
Psalm 125:2

Many years ago, I made a decision to follow Christ. My heart was fixed and my mind was made up. I did not halt between two opinions. I knew that God was God and I was committed to serving Him.

One night as I entered the pulpit under the tent, I found a note. I picked it up and read it. The note said, *"Shut up or get thrown in the canal!"* I ignored both options and took my own. I stood boldly for the name of Christ. The Gospel I preached was accepted by some and rejected by others. Nevertheless, God was with us. Clearly, the person who threatened me rejected the Gospel. I never found out who sent the threat, but God did not allow me to be thrown into the canal.

Repeatedly I was threatened and repeatedly God protected me. I was doing His Will and walking in His anointing. God moved on the heart of an unsaved man who became my personal self-appointed bodyguard. He never had to say or do anything. His very presence at the tent meetings was enough. However, we must remember that the devil works overtime attacking the saints.

One night while I was preaching, someone placed a ball of cotton and matches in my gas tank. As I preached under the anointing of God, the Holy Spirit revealed to me what had happened. I walked to my car, removed the cotton and matches, came back and finished the message. After service, I drove home without incident.

The truth of the matter is that we have but one option; to obey God. And God will watch over His Word to perform it. When you know that God has called you, you will obey the Call, regardless of the consequences.

THERE WILL BE NO CHURCH

*For I know the thoughts that
I think toward you,
saith the Lord, thoughts of peace, and not of
evil, to give you an expected end.
Jeremiah 29:11*

As a man of God, spiritual unity has always been one of my primary goals. In 1958, God gave me a vision to build a church. So we purchased a plot of land on Hartrey Avenue in Evanston, Illinois. We carefully selected that site because the area was integrated. An integrated neighborhood would cultivate a diversified church. However, Evanston City Officials said, *"You cannot build here because the area is not zoned for a church building."* We had already purchased a house at 1136 Hartrey with plans to use the additional grounds as a parking facility.

The church had a vision and we ran with it. When news of our plans reached the citizens of Evanston, neighbors far and near signed petitions against building a church on Hartrey. We were denied permission to build on that particular site. It would appear that the enemy had won. But, God blessed the sale of the land. The same plot of land that was purchased for $3,000 was sold for $8,500. We retained the house at 1136 Hartrey. It provided rental income for the church. The profit from the sale enabled us to purchase a plot of land on the northwest side of the city, at 1932 Dewey Avenue, now also known as Bishop Carlis L. Moody Avenue. This location continues to be the home of Faith Temple Church of God in Christ at Evanston.

So do not get discouraged when doors are closed in your face. Do not lose heart when you are ridiculed, laughed at, and told that it cannot be done. Though the vision tarries, wait for it; for if God gave it, it shall surely come to pass.

Later, God revealed who initiated the petition to prevent the church building on Dewey avenue. The petitioner became very ill and was diagnosed with cancer. Her condition required a nurse. The nurse, Sister Adrene Collins, was a member of our congregation. As she cared for the woman, she made bedside confessions. She admitted to Sister Collins that she was the one who initiated the petition to prevent the building of our church. She wanted to depart this life in peace so she requested to meet with me. During my visit, I listened as she confessed her actions to block the church's construction. She asked for forgiveness, I forgave her, and she was able to depart this life, in peace.

The devil is defeated, but he does not stop trying. There were others who petitioned against the church, but they too were defeated. What shall we then say to these things? If God be for us, who can be against us?

In 1959, we did not set up the tent. Instead, we joined Brother A. A. Allen. At that time his tent was the largest in the world, even larger than Barnum and Bailey's Circus tent. During the services, I played the piano while Elder Goldsberry's choir sang. God used us to bring blacks and whites together. While fellowshipping with Brother Allen, he offered $125.00 a week and a trailer home if I would accompany him as he traveled to minister. I told him, *"I believe in my heart that I should stay with the church."* He replied, *"If you really feel that way, I won't ask you anymore."* Even though I was disillusioned with the church and really wanted to go, God did not lead me in that direction. And today I am glad that I stayed.

Although infrequent, I still had the privilege of traveling with Brother Allen. Once, I traveled to Dallas to assist him. After the long train ride, I was refused hotel accommodations and service at the restaurants, because I was black. During that time, segregation ruled. We searched for a place where both of us could eat. Finally, we found a 'greasy spoon' restaurant that must have offered laundering services as well or had done their own laundry. A clothesline hung directly down the middle of the restaurant. I ordered a beef sandwich knowing that I did not like beef. I covered it with an excessive amount of mustard so that I could not taste it. As we ate, I marveled at God. I thought, *"Here is a great big preacher sitting in a 'greasy spoon' with me, when he could have eaten at all of the places that rejected me."*

Since I could not get hotel accommodations, Brother Allen gave me his trailer home and rented a room in the hotel. He also went to the grocery store and purchased enough food for my stay. At the end of my trip, he flew me home on a jet. It was my first jet ride. I returned home ready to resume the work of my ministry.

HAIRCUT OR WORSHIP

For where two or three are gathered together in
my name, there am I in the midst of them.
Matthew 18:20

During the winter of 1959, we had services in a building
behind a barbershop on Church Street. The building
was located at 1821 Church Street, the 'colored' section
of town. It was one and a half blocks long and sat directly
across the street from the Evanston Township High
School. It was called 'The Block'. In addition to the
barbershop, there was a soul food restaurant operated
by Brother Robert Gill, Mother Maggie Gill's late
husband, a neighborhood corner store, and Morrison's
drug store. These were accessible to colored folks. On
the south side of the street was Monticarlo's drug store,
the hangout for the white kids from Evanston Township
High School.

Our church was very small. There were no windows
and only one bathroom, which we shared with the
barbershop's employees, patrons, and loiterers. Needless
to say, the bathroom was not very sanitary. Sometimes
the loiterers left opened whiskey bottles and refuse in
the bathroom, which added to its untidiness. During the
winter it was so cold in the building that the saints kept
their boots and coats on during service. Even though
there was a stove in the building, the inside temperature
seemed to be as cold as outside. The saints were not

discouraged because of these hard times. They persevered knowing that God was faithful and true. There were times when Mother Maggie Logan, Sister Johnnie Hicks and Sister Cammie Ross stayed in that cold uncomfortable building for three days and nights. They were shutting in with the Lord. During the shut-ins, Mother Logan and I alternated leading prayer. While one prayed, the other person rested.

God began to increase the church membership. He sent saints who loved the ministry. Mother Freedom was not an official member of our church, but she loved the ministry and prayed for it regularly. One hour every Sunday she would come and stand outside in the cold and pray for the church.

In 1968 a sister in Christ, Sister America, came to the United States from Santo Domingo. She came to get married and then return to her homeland. She did not speak English, but every Sunday, even when there was no service, she came to Faith Temple and prayed that God would send men to the church. There were three or four men in attendance at that time, but when Sister America prayed, God answered.

It never fails, when God begins to bless, the devil tries to stir up trouble. Some people did not believe that the church was progressing at an acceptable pace, so again, I was asked, *"Are you sure that God sent you here?"* I answered, *"Yes, He did."* Shortly after the murmuring and complaints, it was as if God said, *"Son, since you've proven yourself and stuck with the church, I'm going to send you some help."* Brother Bonapart, Brother Robinson, and Brother Hoffman had been with me since 1958. But God sent Brother William Hicks and a number of other brothers to strengthen the work. Brother Calvin Hudson was one of our first trustees, but he did not remain active and faithful to the service of the Lord.

Our experiences behind the barbershop were many. Demons were cast out and healings occurred. Sister Florence Johnson and her sister Marvell Grace joined Faith Temple after their pastor threatened to put them out of the church for visiting us. Sister Florence experienced dizziness due to anemia. One Sunday, the Holy Spirit told Mother Hudson to ask Florence to remove her gloves so that she could look at her fingernails. They examined her nail beds and cuticles. From the evidence of good blood circulation, they knew that Jesus had healed her. Since then she no longer suffered from low blood.

During the early days, Sister Lucy Steele was over the Sunshine Band. We had quite a few little ones to work with. There were nine church families with small children. In addition, a number of the church mothers, such as, Mother Hudson, brought their grandchildren to the services also. My wife and I interacted with the children often so we could maintain their interest in church. We held Easter egg hunts by the lake and sleepovers at our house. Elder John Brewer, his sisters, and the Roebucks, were all teenagers at the same time, so they fellowshipped together. On Saturday afternoons, John would bring them all on the train to our house in North Chicago to play with our children. They spent the night with us and then we brought them to Sunday school and returned them to their families.

As the church began to grow, I wanted to pastor members of all nationalities. I had always wanted an integrated church and we had several non-blacks. Sister Mildred Baker and Brother Jerry Sodoman joined us. Sister Mildred was confined to a wheelchair so Brother Jerry brought her to the services. We also fellowshipped with other integrated ministries. We worked with Brothers Steve and John Stultz in Chicago, sons of Bob Stultz, founder of 'Prevention Incorporated'.

They were the only whites for miles on the west side of Chicago. They were constantly ridiculed because the black community felt that they did not belong. One day, for no reason at all, some young black boys twisted John's arm out of the socket, put a gun to his mother's head and threatened them. Despite all of that, they stayed because they knew that the Lord had placed them there.

Likewise, I believe that God strategically placed members in my ministry. Sister Maggie Gilmore and her mother, Mother Maggie Tutwiler, affectionately known as Mama Tut, had been members of our church since 1960. Sister Gilmore had previously worked in Bishop Page's office, so she knew 'Who Was Who'. When I did not know who to invite to our church to preach, she helped me. If I mentioned getting a preacher whom she knew something negative about, she would advise against it, but would give me the name of someone else that she felt was more suitable. She gave me directions in selecting ministers because she knew the gospel that I preached and where I stood on certain issues. I never believed that she was bias with her recommendations. One time she said to me, *"There's a young man in Chicago, Elder Randolph Moore, he would be a good speaker."* I told her that I had to think about it.

Some time later, Sister Maggie again asked whether Elder Moore could come and I consented. When he came he had just completed a 40-day fast. The only other person that I knew which would fast so extensively was, my assistant, Brother Jamison. When Elder Moore began to preach, he got all under my skin and God knitted our souls together. He has been with us ever since. When Dr. Moore was scheduled to come to us, he usually arrived late. The church was usually packed to capacity but they were always willing to wait for him. When he got there, he preached so well that we soon forgot that we were angry with him for being late.

In the earlier days, we also fellowshipped with Elder Preston Barrett. Elder Barrett had an encouraging testimony. He was a tap dancer who worked on a showboat on the Mississippi River. In those days you were 'very special' if you were allowed to dance for Caucasians. But one day the Lord saved Elder Barrett. He was mopping the church floor when God filled him with the Holy Spirit. The mop went one way while he went the other. Afterwards, he became an even better dancer in the Holy Ghost as he danced before the Lord on one foot. Shortly afterwards, he left the showboat. His conviction would not allow him to *showboat* at night and go to church on Sunday. So he chose to dance for the Lord.

Once you really get saved, Christ talks with you. When you go to the wrong place, Jesus says, *"You really shouldn't be here."* Why? Because you represent Jesus everywhere you go. God has set certain standards for His people. The people of God are called to a much higher standard than that of the world. We must live by the higher standard that God has called us to.

In 1960, we set up the tent again. During each tent meeting, Walter Perrin and his brother were in attendance. They did not come to hear the Word of God preached, but rather, to protect the preacher. They sat on the trunk of their cars watching over me as I preached. Because I had been threatened previously, they appointed themselves as my new bodyguards. I was amazed how God placed a love for me in the hearts of unsaved men. They were at every meeting until 1962 when I stopped having tent meetings.

In 1961, when I conducted my third revival I noticed that my method of preaching had changed. I did not 'tune-up' my sermons. In a tuned up sermon, you simply sang while you told the story. I do not know why or how it happened, but I started preaching more expository messages. An expository message was much more difficult, but the Holy Spirit taught me. I began to preach deliverance and healing and I soon lost the song. The first area we exercised our deliverance ministry in was employment. Since I had first-hand experience in God blessing me with jobs, I prayed in faith and the people received jobs. Behind the Barbershop, God proved that He truly was in our midst.

FROM DRUGS TO SALVATION

...He that winneth souls is wise.
Proverbs 11:30

From 1967 to 1980, we were actively involved in various outreach ministries. They were designed to win drug addicts to Christ. They included 'Addicts for Jesus', 'Prevention', and 'Street Evangelism'. These ministries reached from the living room of my home to established drug rehabilitation centers to the streets of Chicago. No matter what we had to do or where we had to go, we were determined to snatch souls from the dark clutches of drug addiction.

Faith Temple Church has been a cultivating soil for many people. Members come and go. Some stay for a short period of time while others remain longer. Nevertheless, they are nurtured well and go on to do great things for the Lord. Elder John Lawrence, an Evangelist from New Jersey often visited our church. He was a motivator. He knew how to get things done and there was always something to do. His ministry included drug addict outreach and door-to-door evangelism. He trained the saints how to effectively minister door-to-door. He was anointed in teaching people how to witness.

For two years, we worked with John Jimenez, founder of the 'Addicts for Jesus' ministry. He and I often ministered to drug addicts together until he relocated to New York. Shortly afterwards, Bob Stultz founded 'Prevention Incorporated'. For thirteen years, Faith Temple was the local church home for 'Prevention' members. Both of these outreach ministries were directed to men on drugs. We used two vans to pick the men up for church. As God blessed the works of our hands, we also started various 'drug awareness' programs within the public schools. While assisting Brother Bob Stultz's drug ministry, 'Prevention Incorporated', we experienced sin in its rawest form. While the primary focus of the ministry was to get men off drugs, Prevention Incorporated was also designed to keep young children off the streets and away from drugs. Brother Bob would take a van of saints from Evanston to Chicago to witness door-to-door. He often took me to Oak Street in Chicago. Everything imaginable was happening there, but we still witnessed. However, if he felt that an area was too rough for me, he would tell me to wait at the door. Sometimes I waited and other times I did not.

Once we went to Monroe Street in Chicago. The area

was slightly rough, but we were on a mission. Brother Bob knocked on a door and they asked, *"Who is it?"* Bob said, *"It's the preacher."* They invited us in and took us into an English style basement. First, we had to pass through three doors. As we walked through, we saw three prostitutes. They said, *"Since we are going to get our fix anyway, we will allow you to make a video of us to show the teenagers why they should not take drugs."* We agreed that this was a good idea. The video could be shown as part of our drug prevention program.

We left there and went to a place known as the drug addict's haven, located on Ogden Street. We witnessed three women prepare their drugs and inject it into their bodies. The first woman placed a rubber band around her arm to prepare her veins for the needle injection, which she administered herself. Because I do not like needles, I could barely stand to watch. My nausea grew worse as I watched the second and third woman. The second lady injected herself in the leg and the third one in the neck. The third woman did not get enough in the needle the first time, so she had the second girl take the needle, wash it, and put more drugs in it. Then the third lady injected herself again. Within a few minutes, she was quite woozy and so was I. I asked the Lord to get me out of there. I did not even want the pictures anymore; I just wanted out of there. I left safely and did not get sick.

With or without videos, we realized that the harvest was truly plentiful and the laborers were few; but the work had to be done. However, 'zeal' for the lost does not always result in 'wisdom' for winning the lost. Nevertheless, we were able to use the pictures in our outreach program.

We held drug prevention seminars in various churches and at Evanston Township High School. We knew the Commander of the Police Department's Evidence Room. He allowed us to take real drugs from the 'lock-up' to show during the presentations. We displayed the drugs in a locked glass case. We also had guys from the recovery program talk about their lives and the effects of drugs in their bodies. We gave real life demonstrations. Soon the 'show-and-tell' had to stop because it had an adverse affect. When the guys relived their experiences, they also revived the spirit, which drove them to start using drugs in the first place. And because of curiosity, some people who had never tried drugs began to try them and were hooked. Godly wisdom directed us to discontinue this particular aspect of the ministry.

THE ELEVENTH HOUR

Then shall ye call upon me, and ye
shall go and pray unto me, and I
will hearken unto you.
Jeremiah 29:12

When you witness the power of God in operation, it compels you to have faith. As a young boy, I traveled with various preachers. In my travels, I accompanied a preacher to a town where a woman sold alcohol and ran the whole town. After the Word of God was preached, the woman received Jesus. The man, who owned the sawmill in town, told the preacher, *"If God can save that woman, you can have whatever you need to build a church."* God is still God!

In the late 1970's I was inspired to start a Christian school. As I walked in obedience to God's directions, the mission was accomplished. In September 1980, Faith Christian Academy opened with an enrollment of 23 students. Within five years, the enrollment grew to almost 100 students. The academic level ranged from kindergarten through eighth grade. All of the faculty members were Christians and qualified in their specialized areas. We were grateful that God chose the people to teach the young minds entrusted in our care. We knew that we could trust Him.

The Faith Christian Academy graduates continued their education in the public school system and/or other parochial schools. When the National Achievement Test were given, most Faith Christian Academy graduates scored as high or higher than other students in their grade level. God truly smiled upon our humble beginning.

We appreciated the dedication and hard work of our faculty members and never wanted to cause them unnecessary hardship. We continually prayed for them and asked God to always allow us to do what was right on their behalf. We consistently prayed that the Lord would enable us to meet the Faith Christian Academy payroll. These were God's people. We did not want their commitment to His work to cause them to suffer more than if they were teaching in the public schools. There were numerous times when the faculty's payday was just around the corner and we did not have the money to meet the payroll. Each time, God came through and supplied the finances.

I remember two specific instances when God used the same woman to meet the payroll without her knowledge of our need. The woman was not a member of Faith Temple, but she visited regularly. Easter Sunday morning, 1990, at the end of the 6:00 a.m. sunrise service, the woman asked to speak to me. They sent my assistant pastor to talk with the lady, but she refused to speak with him. Again she asked to speak with me. She said, *"I have to talk to Bishop."* I went to see what the lady wanted. She said, *"Bishop, the Lord told me to give you this."* She gave me a check for $3,000. This woman had no way of knowing that we needed exactly $3,000 for Monday morning's payroll, but God did.

On another occasion we needed $5,000 to pay the teachers. We did not have the money. However, early that morning, we wrote the checks. My wife and I placed the checks on the table and prayed over them. We left them there and waited on the Lord. Later that afternoon, an anonymous certified check, in the amount of $5,000, was delivered to us. The name of the purchaser was whited out. The certified check was a miraculous timely answer to prayer. We were able to issue our payroll checks at 2:00 p.m., our normal disbursement time, one-hour before school was dismissed. Later, we found out that it was the same woman who had given me the $3,000 check.

If you trust God, you do not make plans *'just-in-case'* He does not come through. We believed that God was going to do it, and if he did not, we would just have to be late. We also knew that we had never been late before, so we decided to trust God. Thanks be unto God who always causeth us to triumph. For sixteen years we were never late with the Faith Christian Academy payroll.

Most of us know that it is difficult for churches to be approved by the zoning board for expansion projects. In 1984, we wanted to add a second floor to the church. We really needed God to work a miracle. We went before the zoning board to present our case. Our appointment was scheduled for 7:30p.m.. The two prior presentations were so extensive that they continued beyond 11:30p.m.. While we were making our presentation, some of the zoning board members fell asleep. When we finished our presentation and it was time to vote, those who were asleep woke up long enough to vote, 'Yea'. We received a unanimous 'Yea', with no questions asked or added mandates. God is all-powerful!

A STREET CALLED MOODY

...go into the street which is called Straight...
Acts 9:11

As in previous years, there was an excitement in the air. The saints were busy secretly planning a Pastor's Appreciation celebration for 40 years in the ministry. Some accused me of snooping, trying to find out what was happening. On some occasions I was guilty, but this time, I was innocent. I had no idea of the plans which were unfolding or of the project they were engaged in. I was taken completely by surprise.

It was Sunday morning and the sanctuary was filled from front to back. Each presenter had a limited amount of time to make their presentation. Several presentations were made, but a specific one was saved for last. It was then announced that the rules governing the previous presentations did not apply to the one that was about to be made. Whatever time was needed would be made available for this announcement. The 'unknown' made me nervous. I did not know what was going on or what would happen next. My wife and I were asked to stand. The presentation was covered and sealed in such a way, that I could not even peek.

I watched as my mother, Geneva Smith, was called to the podium to do the unveiling. My mother had been very ill and just resumed attendance to church. The ushers escorted her to the podium and she stood there as instructed. At that time, I did not know that she had no idea what was going on either; she blindly followed. When Sister Rena finished reading the overview of historical facts, the final decree read, *"An Honorary Street Named, 'Bishop Carlis L. Moody Avenue', will be placed along with the 'Dewey Avenue' street sign."* This is the street where Faith Temple Church of God in Christ at Evanston is located. I could not contain myself or the emotions that followed.

The committee had gone to the Mayor of the city of Evanston and requested that I be bestowed such an honor. Sister Carolyn Hollins played a major role in this accomplishment. This had never been done in the city before, much less for a living honoree. Honorary street names were usually done after a person was deceased. My mind could not comprehend the favor that God had granted me. I, Carlis Lee Moody, Sr., a boy from Tifton, Georgia, who came from a broken home, the product of single-parenting, was now the **first** living person in Evanston, Illinois, to receive such an honor. Even today, I am overwhelmed as I behold with my eyes the wondrous works of God.

Only God knew that this appreciation service would be the last one my mother would share with me. God ordained that she be there to behold such an honor of distinction and present it to the son of her womb.

A SONG FOR THE PASTOR

Sing unto him a new song...
Psalm 33:3

Sister Rena Ranger asked Elder Edward Jackson to sing the sermonic solo for one of the Pastor's Appreciation services. Since he had a month to prepare, he petitioned the Lord, specifically, for a song about me. However, he did not want to mention my name. Upon hearing the song, he wanted people to recognize who it was about. Inasmuch as Elder Jackson made a specific request, God answered him specifically. The Holy Spirit stirred up his mind, reminding him of one of my favorite expressions, "What does the Book say?" Within twenty-four hours of the thought, the Lord breathed the song into Elder Jackson's spirit: "What does the Book say?"

During the solo, I was moving from side to side just enjoying the song, when suddenly I identified with the words. I then realized that he was singing about me. I was overwhelmed by the special way God blessed me through a song. In answer to Elder Jackson's prayer, the people immediately recognized that the song was about me and they loved it. The choir immediately picked up the melody. The saints joined in and were blessed by the song also.

When Sister Ranger asked me for permission to make the song available to the saints, I happily gave my approval. To that end, a compact disc recording of the song entitled, "What Does The Book Say" was produced.

What Does The Book Say

I know a man of integrity,
he is a man much like you and me.
But when it comes to the Word of God,
he won't compromise.
He preaches the word most everywhere,
around the world he has been there.
And when it comes to the Son of God,
he will not deny.

Now I'll follow him as he follows Christ,
if I want to see God I've got to live right.
And when I ask him why are things the way they are,
he always says

What does the Book say?
What does the Bible say?
For the Word of God has always been,
and remains the bottom line.
What does the book say?
What does the Bible say?
For the answers to this life,
we must turn to God's Word every time.

He teaches the saints to be their best,
that we can all walk in holiness.
He says the true man is revealed,
when he's all alone.
I thank you Lord for giving him,

thank you Lord for the life he lives.
I'll follow on in what I've learned,
till you call me home.
I can hear him say,

What does the Book say?
What does the Bible say?
For the word of God has always been,
and remains the bottom line.

What does the book say?
What does the Bible say?
For the answers to this life,
we must turn to God's word every time.

Now when I think of his legacy,
he has touched the lives of you and me.
And I know there is no doubt,
who I'm talking about.
Now I have a wife and I have a home,
and I have children of my own.
Now when they ask me why the world Is this way,
I smile and say
(Repeat Chorus)

RECORDING ENSEMBLE:

Kenneth L. Daniel, Sr.

Le'Trisha A. Daniel

Ashley Dozier

A. Lavern Gregory

Edward E. Jackson

Kahla Jackson

Selma Jackson

Arnett Judon

Sherren Lewis

Aurelia M. Milam

Elizabeth H. Moody

Rebecca L. Moody

Shelley R. Moody

Vicki L. Moody

POWERFUL MEMORIES

*...These that have turned the
world upside down...
Acts 17:6b*

As I look back over my life, it's the 'memories' that keep me going in the right direction. They help me remain focused, but they are never a substitute for the Word of God. I remember that as a child, my grandparents were a part of the Church of God in Christ. However, I also remember receiving Christ at age nine under a pastor who was no longer a part of the Church of God in Christ.

When I first moved to Illinois, Brother Willie Walker introduced me to a local Church of God in Christ assembly. He took me to visit a church pastored by Elder James W. Markham. Elder Markham was my pastor from 1952 through 1956. He was affectionately called 'Dad Markham'. Dad Markham was a praying man. I often visited him on the weekends. During my visits, I simply sat at his feet while he taught me the Word of God. In the afternoon he would pray. I would sometimes fall asleep while he prayed and when I awoke he was still praying. He taught me what it meant to live holy.

In 1952, Dad Markham introduced me to Bishop Louis Henry Ford during the organization of the First Jurisdiction of Central Illinois. I observed Bishop Ford's life and admired his strength in leadership. I also respected his tenacity. Bishop Ford died in 1995.

However, the faith he had in me and the care he showed me lives on.

Bishop Charles Harrison Mason founded the Church of God in Christ organization. He was respectfully and affectionately called 'Dad Mason'. In 1906 Dad Mason traveled from Texas to Azusa Street in Los Angeles, California, where he received the Baptism of the Holy Ghost. In 1907, he established the Church of God in Christ organization in Lexington, Mississippi. The church taught integration. People of all nationalities came to what was known as 'the place of power'. It did not matter who you were; everyone embraced and loved each other. However, it was understood that men did not embrace ladies, especially Black men with Caucasian ladies.

During 1906-1914, Dad Mason was granted a charter to ordain ministers. Black and White ministers came to Dad Mason for their ordination. In 1914, the Caucasian brothers separated themselves and formed their own charter. Their meetings were held in Topeka, Kansas.

In 1955, I started attending the National Church of God in Christ Convocation which is annually held in Memphis, Tennessee at the end of the harvest season. This meeting is the national convention for all members within the Church of God in Christ. Our national headquarters is located in Memphis, Tennessee.

In the early fifties, Blacks were not allowed to stay in the hotels. Hence, the saints had to find accommodations in various homes. Because of our large attendance, it was difficult to find enough sleeping arrangements, so they slept in shifts. Some went to church while others slept. The owners of the houses would change the bed linen during the rotation. This cycle continued throughout the entire convention. Each person was always sufficiently refreshed. Those were days of strong commitment and great endurance.

This continued until Dr. Martin Luther King marched in Memphis on behalf of the garbage workers. The march was not against the hotels, but it opened the doors to justice and equality. Bishop Louis Henry Ford seized the opportunity. He gathered a group of saints, went to City Hall, and presented our racial discrimination case. The remaining saints interceded in prayer. As a result, Bishop Ford was the first black to stay in the Peabody Hotel.

I had the privilege of fellowshipping with Dad Mason for six years. The first time I saw him was the year I was married. He was over 90 years old and still casting out devils. He did not yell. He simply spoke the Word of God in faith. I remember when a woman passed out in the doorway of the Temple. They picked her up and sat her in front of Bishop Mason. He took some blessed oil, tapped her on the head, and called the devil out by name. It was amazing to see someone who was lifeless, arise as if they had awaken from a deep sleep. As she began praising God, tears streamed down my face as I stood in amazement at God's power.

Times were hard, but Dad Mason built the National

Headquarters Temple in Memphis out of bricks and steel. He accomplished this during a time when steel was in short supply. In fact, it was exclusively reserved for the military. Dad Mason realized that adverse situations are no barrier for God. Despite the restrictions, God made a way for Dad Mason to purchase steel and build a Temple.

Dad Mason was used by God through many gifts. Brother Jairus Pratcher was blind, but when Bishop Mason touched him on the forehead, by the power of the Holy Ghost, Mr. Pratcher received his sight. I never heard Dad Mason say, *"I have this gift or I have that gift"*, he directed all glory back to God.

Hardship or adversity did not trouble Bishop Mason. One time, he walked into a room with two thousand men arguing, and said, *"Get on your knees and let's pray."* When he said, *"Let's pray"*, he meant let's pray. He believed that if you argued for four hours you could pray for six hours. Some of the preachers did not want to pray, so they would watch Dad Mason. When his eyes were closed, they slipped out.

Bishop Mason was a man of profound wisdom and sometimes he was rather humorous. During one of the meetings, a sister told him that if she did not speak, she would burst. He rebuked her and told her to sit down. He said, *"You may get angry, but you are not going to bust."* I learned from how he handled situations that prayer should always precede your actions.

Another great influence in my life was the power of

God I witnessed among women. The sisters met every Tuesday for prayer and Bible study. During a midday service, some of the sisters encircled a woman who had a tumor. Her stomach was as large as an expecting mother. The sisters laid hands on her stomach, prayed in faith, and God removed the cancer. When the preacher arrived, the lady was healed, because signs follow them that believe. Wherever there is real Bible faith in God, He always answers.

Brother A. A. Allen was also very instrumental in my spiritual growth. In 1958, Brother Allen conducted a summer revival at 73rd Street and Cicero Avenue in Chicago, Illinois. Signs and wonders followed the Word of faith that he preached. Double lines circled the inside of the tent with those that needed prayer. People with all types of diseases, ailments, and sicknesses came from far and near. Sometimes, when the Spirit moved, Brother Allen would just touch each person in the line as he ran pass. One night the police came, arrested him, and took him to jail. They charged him with 'practicing medicine without a license', because blind eyes were opened, and the sick were healed. When they arrested Brother Allen, Brother Robert Shambach stepped up and carried the service on.

These are but a few treasured memories I share with you.

THE MISSIONARY

Mission Produces Miracles

COUNTRIES WHERE BISHOP MOODY
PREACHED OR VISITED

Preached

HAITI	COLUMBIA	INDIA
JAMAICA	CANADA	SRI LANKA
MEXICO	PHILIPPINES	GHANA
PANAMA	SINGAPORE	MALAWI
BELIEZE	KOREA	SOUTH AFRICA
DOMINICAN REPUBLIC	BRAZIL	KENYA
PUERTO RICO	CUBA	ITALY
TRINIDAD	SWEDEN	GERMANY
ST. THOMAS	FINLAND	JAPAN
BARBADOS	ENGLAND	BELGIUM
BERMUDA	NORWAY	NIGERIA
BAHAMAS	ISRAEL	CAICOS & TURKS ISLAND

Visited

FRANCE

EGYPT

CHINA

THIALAND

MALAYSIA

The harvest is plentiful, the laborers are few, but Bishop Moody carries the good news of the Gospel to Belize.

Brother Chuck Rivers with the youth on a mission team, tells the Chile Saints what to expect during their time of fellowship.

In Dominica Republic, Bishop Moody is ready to make music unto the Lord.

There is hunger in the land of Ethiopia for bread and milk, but also for the Word of God.

Bishop Moody is getting ready to tour a military helicopter in Germany.

Although Germany is not an impoverished country, Bishop Moody preaches with the same diligence and conviction.

Bishop Moody takes the Word of God to the market place of Haiti.

The children of Kenya, East Africa look on as Elder Darrell Hines smiles for the camera.

The young Elder Hines (now Bishop) accompanied Bishop Moody to this mission field.

The saints of Malawi walks away with smiles after Bishop Moody and Elder Lyle Foster ministered the Word of God.

The unity of the brotherhood
in the Philippines as
(left) Bishop Louis Spencer of
Buffalo, New York, Bishop Moody
and (right) Bishop Photo of the
Philippines stand together.

In Santo Domingo, Bishop Moody
stands with Johnny Philepi, the
brother whom God used in his first
trip outside of the U.S. and
Sister America who was a faithful
intercessor for Faith Temple, asking
God to send men to the church.

Pillars of strength during the
South African soul outreach;
Elder Derrick Flynn and friend
with Bishop Moody.

*The saints of South Africa
pressing inward and standing
in the doorway just to worship and
hear the Word of God preached.*

*The accolades of the energetic
Missionary Sandra Parker
in South Africa, again causes
Bishop Moody to "Shy Away!"*

*The children of Uganda Christian
School stand wondering
whether they will be able
to continue their educaion.
The government is requiring a
stronger building to be built.
Money is needed.*

Helen Wamala (far right) stands with former moslem women who converted to Christianity, as they offer their talent of handcrafting to God.

Bishop Louis Henry Ford looks on as Bishop Moody delivers the Word of God.

Bishop Moody kneeling beside a portrait of Bishop Charles Harrison Mason. Bishop Moody appears to be leaning on Bishop Mason's knee and his shoulder behind Bishop Mason's arm.

*Bishop Moody appointed
President of Missions.*

*Bishop Moody stands with
Reverend DuPlesi,
who introduced Pentecost to the
Catholic church.*

*Bishop Moody and
Dr. Cho of South Korea,
Pastor of the largest church in
the world with over 100,000 members.*

*From left to right.
Bishop P.A. Brooks, Elder Vasquez (father),
Bishop Moody, and Elder Vasquez (son);
father and son are from Santiago, Chile.*

I remember Mama in a very special way.

No Way Out

Is any thing too hard for the Lord?...
Genesis 18:14

In 1982 I hosted a tour group of seventy-two people to the Pentecostal World Conference in Nairobi, Kenya. On the way to Kenya, we traveled to Israel and Egypt. We were looking forward to wonderful experiences in each country. While in Israel, I preached in Caiphas's house and some of the group was baptized in the Jordan.

We prepared to leave Israel for Egypt. In order to get from Israel to Egypt, we had to ride a ferry or drive across a bridge. We traveled from Jerusalem by bus to the Suez Canal. By the time we arrived at the Suez Canal, the last ferry had already crossed into Egypt and the bridge was drawn. There was no way in until the next morning.

The saints began to pray. About two hours passed. As they prayed, a man came along the Suez Canal bank. I explained our situation and he left to find someone to reconnect the bridge. A short time later, both of our buses crossed over into Egypt. We spent four days in Cairo.

As we prepared to go to Nairobi, Kenya for the Pentecostal World Conference, we were told that the airline, EL AL Airlines, was on strike. The airline officials told Elder J.W. Denny & Elder John Lawrence that there was no way to get out of Egypt. They also told them that our tickets were not transferable to any other airline, because EL AL was a government-controlled airline. Again, the saints began to pray.

About two hours later, an official from the main office told us that they had changed their mind and would allow one plane to fly, even though they were still on strike! Not only did this plane carry all of us from Egypt to Nairobi, Kenya, but it also stopped in Jerusalem and picked up a group from Canada who was also enroute to the conference in Nairobi.

After staying in Kenya for a week, EL AL Airlines was still on strike. God allowed Swiss Air airlines to accept our tickets so the entire group could get home. To God be the Glory!

I'M ON HIS MIND

But He knoweth the way that I take:
when He hath tried me,
I shall come forth as gold.
Job 23:10

God's ways and methods are unsearchable, but He always has our best interest at heart. Whatever He's doing or saying, it's for His glory and our expected end. The first trip I ever took outside of the country was to Dominican Republic on January 26, 1970. This was almost six years before I was appointed International

President of the Home and Foreign Missions Department of the Churches of God in Christ.

In June 1969 I met Johnny Philepi, a native of the Dominican Republic. He was a preacher currently residing in the United States. I invited him to visit our church. I gave him the name and address of the church and thought nothing else about it. He later visited and became a member. At the end of each Service, he asked me to minister in Santo Domingo. Finally, I agreed to go and he accompanied me.

We arrived at the Santo Domingo airport on a Monday evening. We were to travel from the airport by rental car. However, I had no rental car reservation, and no cars were available. We joined in prayer. Shortly thereafter, we were informed that someone had reserved a car, but did not show up for it. At the point of need, God provided us with a car. Praise God!

As we began our journey, the traffic was redirected. Because of the detours we decided to go to Johnny's home in San Pedro de Macoris. Since Johnny knew the owners of the local radio station, we stopped and he asked if they would permit us to do a spiritual broadcast. Arrangements were made for us to preach on the air every morning from 6:00 to 7:00 a. m.. We agreed that each of us would preach one-half hour, and he would also serve as my translator. For the next nineteen days, we preached under the anointing of the Holy Ghost.

During my time in the Dominican Republic, twenty churches were added to the Church of God in Christ organization. God was preparing me for a work of such magnitude, that I could never have imagined. The work, which began more than thirty-five years ago, is still going strong.

I returned to the Dominican Republic to preach at a church in Santo Domingo. I had ministered in Santo Domingo on other occasions so I knew how to navigate around the surrounding cities. My hotel was in a city more than thirty-seven miles from the church. I rented a car for my commute.

The language barrier did not hinder the move of the Holy Spirit. As the preached Word was translated, many believed on the Lord Jesus Christ and accepted Him as their personal Saviour. Testimonies were given of the transforming power of God. Although I could not understand what the translator said, my spirit bore witness.

One evening while driving back to my hotel, the blackness of the night suddenly gripped me. It was midnight. The reality of traveling alone in the darkness, unable to speak the language, became very frightening. I hoped and prayed that there would be no reason for me to get out of the car. I was in a grassy area, surrounded by the ocean. As I drove, I could hear the cracking sound of crabs, which had covered the road, being crushed beneath my tires. Suddenly, out of the darkness two policemen flagged me down. I was frightened but I pulled over and waited. I did not get out because it was so dark. Besides, I knew that I could not speak

Spanish. I reached into my pocket to get my driver's license (something you wouldn't dare do today because they would assume you were reaching for a gun) and handed it to them. As they examined it, the Spirit of the Lord overshadowed me with laughter. I laughed hysterically. Then the policemen began to laugh. They too became hysterical with laughter, handed me my driver's license, and sent me on my way. As they walked away, I drove off as fast as I could without looking back. The Word of God says that a merry heart doth good like a medicine, and I'm a witness that laughter can set you free. To this day, I have no idea why the policemen stopped me. I returned to my hotel, went to my room and knelt to pray, thanking God for his protection. I remained in Santo Domingo for another week. I continued to travel alone on the dark roads. God had given His angels charge over me.

BLIND FAITH

...observe all things whatsoever I have commanded you: and, lo, I am with you always, even unto the end of the world...
St. Matthew 28:20b

Brother Joye Varogeze was a native of India, who had come to the United States to visit his brother, Zechariah in Bible school. Brother Zechariah introduced me to

Brother Joye. Because of his Bible school affiliation, Brother Zechariah was known throughout the State Missions conference. My fellowship with Brother Joye led to a lasting relationship. A few years later, Brother Joye served as a teacher at Faith Temple's Bible school.

For approximately two years, Brother Joye requested that I visit India. In 1972, I agreed to go. A few days before we were scheduled to leave, Brother Joye came to my home crying and told me that he could not accompany me as planned. The government had confiscated his passport and he could not leave the States. They were conducting an investigation. I promised the Lord that if he provided the money, I would go and do the work. So when Brother Joye informed me that he was detained, without hesitation, I told him I would go alone.

Since we planned to travel together and he was to be our guide, I had no information about the trip. Nor did I have details of our mission duties. All I knew was that I promised him I would go. Neither he nor I thought about the information I would need since he was unable to travel. I left the States knowing only the destination on my airline ticket. I did not know if anyone would be waiting for me when I arrived and I had never been to India before.

We landed in Bombay, India and discovered that my luggage was left in New York. Since Bombay was a port of entry, I could not board my connecting flight. I had to stay in Bombay until my luggage arrived. The airport authorities determined that my luggage was on the next flight. All I could do was wait. I walked outside of the airport and stood looking towards the sun, not praying, nor planning, just wondering. While I was standing there, someone tapped me on my shoulder and said, *"Sir, it looks like you are stranded and have problems. Can I help you?"* I turned and there was an Indian man standing beside me. I explained my situation to him and he offered to take me to a hotel to rest. During the drive to the hotel, we talked. When we arrived and I finished registering, the stranger said to the agent, *"If he's unable to pay, I'll return in two days and pay the debt."* The stranger went his way and I was taken to my room.

The weather was extremely hot, 118° degrees Fahrenheit. I was thirsty and wanted some cold water. When I got to my room, I ran the water until it was very cold, filled a big tall glass to the brim, and quickly gulped it down. After twenty-six hours of travel, the water tasted good. So I drank a second glass. After that, I began to feel refreshed and very satisfied. Then I looked up and saw a sign over the mirror, which read, *"DO NOT DRINK THE WATER"*. The Holy Spirit did not allow me to panic. He immediately brought to my spirit, Mark 16:18, *"If they drink any deadly thing, it shall not hurt them."* With that, I took a shower, put on my pajamas, and went to sleep. After several hours I awoke and returned to the airport to get my luggage. I never saw the stranger who cared for me again.

After I picked up my luggage and received my clearance, I boarded the next flight to Calcutta. When I got on the plane no one was sitting beside me, so the flight attendant asked if I would be willing to change my seat so that a family could sit together. I agreed and she directed me to a seat next to an Indian man. I introduced myself as Brother Moody. During our conversation I learned that the man was a preacher. He asked me where I was headed. I could not pronounce the city, so I showed him my ticket. He told me that there were no flights going to Bubaneshwa that night. He then asked me if I had made reservations for a hotel. I softly replied, "*No*". He gave me the name of a hotel and told me to take the airport van to the office where they would give me the address. He also informed me that the airport van ride was complimentary.

When I arrived at the airport office, it was closed. There was a Caucasian woman standing in the doorway, waiting for the arrival of a visiting group from America. The group should have been on the same bus that I was on, but they were not. We began to talk. I soon found out that she was a missionary from Chicago, Illinois, currently living in Calcutta. She asked me why I was there. Although I had very little details, I told her that I was on a mission. I asked her about the hotel that I was trying to locate. She concluded that the Lord sent her to pick me up, especially since her group did not arrive. The missionary told the driver to place my luggage into the car and they took me to the hotel. During our conversation, I discovered that she was a member of the Judson Baptist Church on the north side of Chicago.

As I registered at the hotel, the missionary decided to see whether any of her visiting group was by chance, at that hotel. The attendant checked and her entire group was registered. She had no way of knowing that they were there since she did not make their hotel arrangements.

The next day, I left Calcutta to continue my journey to Bubaneshwa. I arrived in Bubaneshwa on Thursday instead of Wednesday. Although I faced many challenges, they delayed me by only one day. I was in India for twenty-one days. I stayed in Bubaneshwa longer than I have ever stayed anywhere.

The investigations against Brother Joye proved to be nothing, except that God wanted to teach me some things. I faced adversities that would not have occurred if my brother had been with me. This increased my trust in God. Within three days, Brother Joye joined me. As iron sharpenth iron, so did our faith join together accomplish a good work for the Kingdom of God.

In 1973, I returned to India to preach. I arrived on Wednesday and was scheduled to leave on Saturday for Colombo, Sri Lanka. However, I missed my connecting flight from Calcutta to Colombo. They told I had to wait until eleven o'clock Monday morning for the next flight. I reminded God that I had to preach on Sunday night. I became sad because I knew that the people would have walked long dusty roads to come to the services. There was no way to communicate my dilemma to them in advance. I prayed to God and I bound the hindrances and obstacles that came to prevent my departure.

Sunday morning, the Holy Spirit spoke and said, *"Go to the airport and verify Monday's flight."* Upon my arrival, I spoke with an airline representative, who confirmed my reservation for Monday. She also informed me that there was a special flight departing today. She said that if I could get my luggage and return by 1:00 p.m., they would put me on the special flight. Needless to say, I returned to the hotel, retrieved my suitcase, which was already packed, and returned in time to catch the flight. I arrived in Colombo Sunday night, ready to preach.

During the service, I preached from Mark 11:22, *"Have Faith in God"*. Because of the culture, I was careful not to speak against any of the gods. However, I was just as careful to preach Jesus and Him crucified. When I finished ministering the Word of God, the people came for prayer in faith, based on the preached Word. Prayer lasted for over two hours. After service a young lady and her husband came to me and said, *"My father is sick, bedridden and cannot walk. Can you come and pray for him that Jesus might heal him?"* The next day I accompanied the couple to their house, prayed the prayer of faith, and God healed him instantly. The sixty-nine year old man rose up and began to walk.

The entire family of nine attended the next service. After the service they gave up the practice of hinduism and made a commitment to serve Jesus. The following Wednesday they were all baptized in the creek. God had an appointment with this family, and He saw to it that I was there on time and in His time.

My third trip to India took me through the back woods of the state of Orrisa. During the eleven days of travel I discovered that all of the water was bad. If you were not a native, the water could make you very ill. My God, whose eyes are in every place, saw my dilemma and spoke to my heart. He led me to drink water with lemon for the duration of the trip. He also instructed me to only eat boiled eggs and mangoes. When I returned home, I had a complete physical examination. I told my doctor what I ate and drank. He verified that it was the best thing I could have done. When the examination was complete, I received a clean bill of health. From my beginning to my eternal rest, my life is hid in Christ, in God.

It seemed that traveling to India 'with clothes' was not a wise thing for me to do. Again I traveled to India, and again my luggage did not arrive. Naturally, the airlines made promises to deliver, but they could only do what was humanly possible. But God, who specializes in the impossible, intervened on my behalf. Since I was concerned and a little disturbed about my clothes, God sent me a word of Prophesy. He promised that my clothes would arrive before I left Brother Jacob's house to return home. I rested in God's promise. Brother Jacob was the 'voice of hospitality' assigned to me while I ministered in India.

We arrived at Brother Jacob's house later that afternoon. His son, David, left for New Delhi unaware that I would arrive without any clothes. However, before leaving home, he laid out underwear, shirts, and socks on his bed, and hung slacks on the door. Even more astounding, we wore the same size clothing. Brother Jacob gave me the liberty to wear what God had prepared for me. My clothes did not arrive until the day I was to return home.

Well, maybe it's not just India. A short time later when I attended the Convocation in Haiti, I had a similar experience. I didn't realize until my arrival that I had left my suit bag at home. Elder Hill, a preacher in the Church of God in Christ organization, also came to the Convocation. He came prepared to bless the people of Haiti. He brought a suitcase filled with suits to give to the needy. But I found myself, as one of the needy in Haiti. When Elder Hill learned of my situation, God gave him grace to help me. The suits were my exact size so he gave me enough suits for the week. I had a different suit to wear each day. At the end of the meeting, I returned all of the suits to Elder Hill.

MY APPOINTMENT

For promotion cometh neither from the east,
nor from the west, nor from the south.
But God is the judge.
Psalm 75:6-7a

In 1968, I worked as a field representative for the Church of God in Christ Missions department. Bishop S. Martin was the President and Bishop Goldsberry was Vice-President.

In 1972, Bishop Martin became a Jurisdictional Bishop and could not occupy both offices. The Missions department was placed under a committee of three people. The Chairman was F. D. Washington and his assistants were C. L. Anderson and J. A. Blake. The three of them served from 1972 until 1975.

In 1975, the Presiding Bishop, Bishop James O. Patterson invited me to come and preach at his church. To any preacher this would have been an honor, and it was. However, unknown to me, the intention of the invitation was for me to be observed and considered for the appointment of Missions President.

In November 1975, I attended the Convocation in Memphis, Tennessee. During the convocation new officers are appointed. I was asked to conduct a meeting with all of the Mission presidents and Mission leaders. Prior to my meeting, Bishop Patterson and his assistants, Bishop Louis Ford and Bishop Washington held a meeting. The following day, Bishop Patterson sent for me. I was in the midst of a meeting, but I graciously excused myself. I joined Bishop Patterson and the General Assembly on the platform. During the General Assembly, Bishop Patterson announced that he was appointing me President of the missions department. I would be President of the missions department for all of the Churches of God in Christ worldwide. I was surprised and shocked, but I humbly accepted the appointment.

As president of the missions department, I oversee all of the churches' mission concerns both domestic and foreign. It has been over thirty years that God has sustained me in this work. I cannot explain the awesome power of God, but this will give you a glimpse of his power. With my extensive travel I have never been bitten by mosquitoes or hot to the point of perspiration. I have slept in tents filled with bats without harm and in rooms where lizards covered the walls. In all these things, God sustained me. I had to preach the Gospel of Jesus Christ. There were souls who needed to be snatched from the hands of the enemy. There were many hungry souls, which needed to be delivered from the damnation of hell.

ACCESS FROM ABOVE

I know thy works: behold, I have set before thee an open door, and no man can shut it...
Revelation 3:8

The Church of God in Christ had become international. My heart rejoiced as I praised God for being a part of an organization that brought glory to Jesus. I was committed to the call of God and willing to do whatever I could to further the Gospel. It could be said that this was a bitter, sweet time. It was 1979 and the presiding Bishop of the Church of God in Christ Organization sent me to Liberia, West Africa to handle church business. During that same year, the African Politicians established the Organization of African Unity, and Liberia became its headquarters.

Several years earlier, the Church of God in Christ Organization appointed a native brother to serve as general superintendent of the churches in Liberia. He was solely responsible for overseeing all the churches in his area. He also ordained and appointed pastors and coordinated the annual church conventions. At this time, however, there were other situations occurring in Liberia that were unknown to the Church of God in Christ headquarters. One day Elder Abraham Brown, a pastor and district superintendent, called me from Liberia. He requested that I come to Liberia and investigate some unethical things that were happening there. The situations had become common knowledge among the people in Liberia. It was known that the brother was using the church as a ploy to defraud the government. He reported that the Church of God in Christ Organization had schools in some places where we had none. He appointed bogus superintendents for the non-existent schools, and then filed papers with the government to get monetary assistance. He completely misrepresented the church.

The Church of God in Christ Organization had sixty-five churches in Africa and over thirty schools in Liberia. Usurping his authority, the brother decided to change the name of the organization from 'Church of God in Christ' to 'United Church of God in Christ'. He was attempting to align the ministry with the Organization of African Unity. He began his campaign of deceit in Liberia and it extended abroad. His campaign brought him to the United States of America. While in the United

States, he visited several groups who readily received and honored him. One group located in Texas presented him with a plaque designating him as Bishop of Liberia for the Church of God in Christ. He proceeded to create a fraudulent certificate appointing himself as Bishop of Liberia. To do this, he had to forge the Presiding Bishop's signature, Bishop James O. Patterson. He returned to Liberia and made full use of the counterfeit certificate and plaque.

When I arrived in Liberia, I was faced with a great mission. It was twofold, first, to strip a Bishop of his counterfeit stripes, and stop him from stealing money from the government in the name of the church. To do this, I had to:

1. Prove that the brother was not a Bishop, and that he was never appointed Bishop by the church; and,

2. Decide whether the churches he separated unto himself were going to stay with him or return to the COGIC Organization.

To accomplish my mission, I had to get an appointment with President Talbert or Vice-President Warner of Liberia. These were the only persons who could have rectified the situation. They were both ministers. This was a sensitive and delicate situation because politics were high on the agenda and the brother was a fellow-countryman. I immediately realized that the final decision made would be based on what was more acceptable, rather than what was right or wrong.

For two weeks I tried to get an appointment to see the President or Vice-President, but the brother hindered all my efforts. He used his followers to prevent me from getting to the President. Then one day the Lord allowed someone to tell the President's cousin about my situation. He was told about my mission, as well as, the alleged fraudulent activities. The President's cousin telephoned me at the hotel and offered me his help. We arranged that he would pick me up from the hotel and proceed from there. He said that he would develop a plan of action to tackle my situation. Since the cousin had seen pictures of me and he knew who I was, there was no reason for us to describe ourselves to each other. He told me that if I went to church with him on Sunday morning, he would get me in to see the President. On Sunday morning, we arrived at church early. He proceeded to strategically arrange the chairs on the platform so that I would be seated next to the President. When he arrived, everything was in place and all I had to do was talk to him. The plan would have worked, but I was too nervous to speak to him. I sat through the entire service and was too afraid to tell the President about my situation, but God intervened. When the time came to sing, the President and I shared the same hymnal. We sang together, but I couldn't bring myself to speak. Time was rapidly passing and finally the cousin came from the opposite end of the platform and said, *"Mr. President, this man is here to see you. His name is Elder Carlis Moody."* The President turned to his secretary and told him to give me an appointment for Wednesday, and to ensure that his car picked me up and brought me to his office.

On Wednesday morning, while the brother's group was waiting to block me at the regular entrance, the President's car brought me in through the President's entrance. When the driver parked the car, we were directly in front of the elevators that led to the President's chamber.

I stepped off the elevator into the oval office and was greeted by the President. At the conclusion of our meeting, he ruled that whoever wanted to go with the brother and whoever desired to remain with the Church of God in Christ could do so at will. Most of the churches remained with the Church of God in Christ along with some of the schools. Since the day of that ruling, all of the churches, except three, have since returned to Church of God in Christ Organization. Bishop Amos Nyema was appointed the new Jurisdictional Bishop.

GOD WILL TAKE CARE OF YOU

...take no thought for your life...
Matthew 6:25

In my teachings, I constantly remind the saints that they don't ever have to worry about themselves because the Lord promised to take care of them. The things that Joseph's brothers plotted and did against him were intended to bring evil, but God wrought good. God never promised to keep us from bad things, but he promised to take care of us at all times. God knows the heart of all men, whether good or evil. He weighs the motives of the heart and the intents of the actions.

I remember well how I became the Jurisdictional Bishop of Germany. I visited Germany every year since 1976 even before it became a Jurisdiction in 1986. During the annual convocation I preached. The saints designated a day for missions and since I was the president of the missions department, I was allowed to raise special missions offerings. Periodically, I encouraged the saints to give to the visionary work of the Presiding Bishop, Bishop Patterson. At that time Bishop Patterson was sponsoring a building fund drive for the Saints Center Complex, located in Memphis, Tennessee. The complex would provide housing for the All Saints University students and other ministries of the church. The Germany Jurisdiction was very supportive in all of the church's endeavors.

In August 1986, I returned to Germany. The purpose of my visit this time was specifically for another building fund drive. On August 10, 1986, in the midst of a meeting with the saints in Germany, the congregation was told that Germany was established as a Jurisdiction and I was appointed Bishop. All of the saints rejoiced that Bishop Patterson had made such a decision. On Sunday morning I was presented to the congregation as the new Bishop of Germany.

When I returned to the United States, I immediately

wrote Bishop Patterson a letter thanking him for appointing me as Bishop of Germany. I also took that opportunity to invite him to our first workers meeting, which was scheduled for January 1987. He immediately wrote back and accepted our invitation.

When the time arrived to go to Germany, Bishop Patterson, Elder A.Z. Hall and Bishop F. D. Washington met me in Chicago and we traveled together. During the Germany Workers Meeting, Bishop Patterson officially installed me as Jurisdictional Bishop of Germany. I am a witness that God will take care of you and perfect everything that concerns you.

GOD WILL USE MAN OR BEAST

And the Lord opened the mouth of the ass,
and she said...
Numbers 22:28

The Word of God is sent out to accomplish whatsoever pleaseth the Father and if you are standing in the way, watch out!

One sunny Sunday morning in August 1997, the Faith Temple family received approximately one hundred and twenty-five Czechoslovakian visitors. It was time for the preaching of the Word. I stood at the podium to preach, but prior to beginning, I welcomed the visitors through a translator. After the 'Welcome Address,' the translator decided that he would relinquish his position to another for the translation of the sermon. Under the anointing of the Holy Ghost, I told the initial translator that he should translate the message. But the man insisted that he only wanted to translate the 'Welcome'. The discussion went back and forth a couple of times, but I was unmovable, so the man finally agreed.

It was later discovered that the man knew nothing about God and did not want to translate His Word. The Holy Spirit knew the heart of the translator and He knew what He wanted to accomplish, and He did just what He wanted to. God's Word will be preached to every person, and then shall the end come. For every knee shall bow and every tongue shall confess that Jesus Christ is Lord to the glory of God the Father. This translator needed to know about God and God used the man's own mouth to inform him.

I had an option to concede and release the man from translating or to hold fast to my request. I believe that when you live and move in the wisdom of God, you will be relentless in whatever direction he takes you. I could have questioned and accepted the translator's refusal to interpret the message, but the Holy Spirit said to me, that he was the one. God is God!

THIS 'SAME' JESUS

Jesus Christ the same yesterday,
and to day, and for ever.
Hebrews 13:8

The church, the ministry and the building were founded on Hebrews 13:8. The building is the Faith Temple Church of God in Christ located at 1932 Dewey Avenue (Bishop Carlis L. Moody Avenue), Evanston, Illinois 60201. Hebrews 13:8 is the theme scripture for the church. There are many translations of this verse, but all conclude that Jesus Christ is the same no matter what, when or where.

The American Standard states, "Jesus Christ `is' the same yesterday and to-day, `yea' and for ever."

Amplified, "Jesus Christ, the Messiah, is always the same, yesterday, today, (yes) and forever (to the ages)."

Contemporary English, "Jesus Christ never changes! He is the same yesterday, today, and forever."

Darby English, "Jesus Christ 'is' the same yesterday, and to-day, and to the ages to come."

This same Jesus...He is the Great I Am! He is Alpha and Omega, the beginning and the end; the first and the last. He is the Author and the Finisher of my faith. When I accepted Jesus Christ as Lord and Saviour, I also accepted all that He was and all that He said. Inasmuch as He is the same, so is His word. He has proven faithful during my walk with Him. From my small beginning until this present time, He has always remained the same. He is All-Sufficient!

Regardless of the circumstances of life or the changes we encounter, Jesus Christ is the same. He is the same as He was before the foundation of the world, when He walked the earth, and even after He ascended into heaven. His word is the same. His word is forever settled in heaven. His love is the same. Just as He unconditionally loved Abraham, Isaac and Jacob yesterday, he loves us today with that same love. His judgments are the same. His word is sharper than any two-edged sword which goes deep within the heart of man. It divides the soul and spirit, the joints and marrow. His word judges our thoughts and attitudes. That same Jesus, through His word shines light on the motives of our hearts.

Jesus Christ is eternal and we should look forward to spending eternality with Him. We have placed our hope and trust in Him, and are confident that He is the same from everlasting to everlasting. This unchangeable Christ lives within the hearts of His people. Since He remains the same, He helps us to become what He has called us to be. When God is with us, He is all that we need. I encourage all who read this book to walk into your destiny and do the things that God has appointed to you. Walk by faith and not by sight, knowing that, "Jesus Christ the same yesterday, and to day, and for ever."